Oct 23, 2007

Linda I will l
you Always

Capser

MW00815406

The Last Rose

A True Celebration of Eternal Life

THOMAS E. PIERCE

THE LAST ROSE: A TRUE CELEBRATION OF ETERNAL LIFE
PUBLISHED BY BRIDGEWAY BOOKS
P.O. BOX 80107
AUSTIN, TEXAS 78758

For more information about our books, please write to us, call
512.478.2028, or visit our website at www.bridgewaybooks.net.

Library of Congress Control Number: 2006940951

ISBN-13: 978-1-933538-85-3
ISBN-10: 1-933538-85-6

10 9 8 7 6 5 4 3 2 1

This book is dedicated to my wife

Jo Ann M. Pierce

My daughter

Lisa Ann Pierce

The other victims of the accident

Corinne J. Schillings

Andrew M. Roccella

Daniel Bentrem

And to

Sarah Bentrem

May each reading of this book serve as another prayer for her recovery.

ACKNOWLEDGMENTS

As you read this book, I think that it will become obvious that none of us accomplish anything alone. The last thing I expected to do in this lifetime was to write a book. It took hundreds of close friends and relatives all telling me to write my stories down to get me started, and to all of you I say thank you.

To those who have allowed me to include their writings and those who have shared their lives with me during the last year and a half, I thank you. I could never have completed this book without you.

Once I completed the book, I turned to my four editors, Bill Austin, Jane Roesner Graves, Dolly Marciano, and Charlene Roesner. The final format is a tribute to them and the many hours they spent making me look and sound better than I am.

The portraits on the back cover were done by David Derex of Westwood, New Jersey. They will hang in the Legacy restaurant when it opens.

I also have to thank my family. Without them I would never have survived all of this. Finally, I have to thank my daughter Kathy and my granddaughters, Kayla and Emily, whose constant love and devotion keep me going.

TABLE OF CONTENTS

PROLOGUE

On March 6, 2004, my wife, Jo Ann, my daughter Lisa, and I were on the water taxi that overturned in Baltimore's Inner Harbor. I lost both of them that day. I do discuss the accident in this book, but this is not a book about the accident. It is a book about the power of love—love between a man and his wife, between a father and his daughters, between a grandfather and his granddaughters, between a man and his family, between a family and their friends, love as we know it and understand it, and love that goes beyond our understanding. But mostly this book is about the love of two women for the entire family of mankind.

I wrote it in the form of a personal letter to each of you, because I wanted it to be personal. When I first wrote this prologue, I realized that there where things that I wanted you to know about the girls that had already been written. I decided to do something totally different and insert these writings into the text of the book. I wanted you to read some of these first so that you would have some idea of what these women were like in life, so that you might better understand their accomplishments in death.

The first, Jo Ann's eulogy, was written by Dr. David B. Rosenburg, her friend and colleague for over thirty years. Lisa's eulogy was written by two of her friends and co-workers from The New Jersey Institute of Technology (NJIT), Karen Quackenbush and David Clurman. The third, an e-mail about Lisa, was written by

1

her best friend, Jane Roesner Graves, from Stony Brook University, who now lives in Kansas. It could have been her eulogy.

Later in the book, I inserted the letter to Lisa written by Henry Q. Zecher, one of the reservists who rescued her that day. It is a very accurate description of what happened that day on the rescue ship, but that is not why I included it. I included it because I think it is a true letter of love, the type of love I am trying to convey to each of you through this book. I also inserted my remarks to Jo Ann's co-workers at Newcomb Hospital, my speech to the reservists the day they received their medals, and an article about Lisa that was printed in the April issue of the *Talking Stick*, the Association of College and University Housing Officers International's (ACUHO-I) magazine. It was written by her friend and speaking partner John D. Stafford.

This is not the only book I created this year. The first one is a collection of everything that was written about the accident that I could find. It includes eulogies, e-mails, newspaper articles, pictures, internet articles, etc. It is almost four inches thick. I also have hours of videotapes to document the accident and many of the things that have happened this year. Doing all this was very therapeutic. My hope is that someday when my granddaughters are older, I will be able to spend time sharing this book with them so they will better understand who Jo Ann and Lisa really were.

I sincerely hope that you enjoy reading this book as much as I enjoyed writing it.

Tom

JO ANN'S EULOGY
Written by Dr. David B. Rosenberg
March 14, 2004

Dear family and friends of Jo Ann and Lisa,

I want to thank Tom, Kathy, and Steve for giving me the privilege of speaking about Jo Ann today. First, I must apologize for not speaking about Lisa. I don't believe that it would be fitting or proper since I didn't know Lisa that well, but I knew her mother and I know her father and her sister, and I have seen the warmth of this family and can attest to their values, so there is no question in my mind that with Lisa's death, we have all lost an exceptional young woman who had yet to fulfill the full potential of her life.

I knew Jo Ann for almost thirty years. She was my colleague; she was my friend. During that time, we spent countless hours together working with the children on Pediatrics at Newcomb Hospital, and in the clinic, and probably even more hours at the hundreds of meetings, conferences, and planning sessions which are required to efficiently run a clinical hospital department. After Jo Ann came over to run our office two and a half years ago, there were even more meetings and shared meals, and times in between patients for informal conversations—and so I thought I knew Jo Ann very well. I saw in her an exceptional person who combined the skills of a highly-trained, caring pediatric nurse with the unique abilities of a natural leader who was able to relate to people in a sensitive manner. She was an inspiration for all with whom she worked. If you put all these attributes together, along with her pleasant demeanor and a warm and loving and loyal-to-the-end personality, you would have the very extra special package that was Jo Ann Pierce. This, then, was the woman I thought I knew so well.

But the tragic events of this past week, and the response to her death by the many people who knew and worked with Jo Ann, and the stories, they began to tell me about her—made me realize that my picture of her was not as complete as I thought. I now know that I didn't fully appreciate how deeply she cared, and how many, many people she touched in so many meaningful ways. She cast a very wide net.

Everyone who knew Jo Ann will tell you that she was a family person—her family came first. She and Tom were partners in every aspect of their lives—from computers to campers; they did everything together and were devoted to each other. Tom said the other day that in thirty-seven years of marriage, there was never a cross word between them, which for the rest of us married folks is hard to believe—but seeing how they were together, I believe him. He was her rock and she depended on him, and he never faltered.

And there are their daughters—Kathy and Lisa. If you mentioned their names to Jo Ann, her face lit up with that wonderful, broad, star-bright smile of hers. She was involved with every aspect of their lives, and the happiness they provided for her can be surpassed only by the delight she showed when talking about or being with her granddaughters, Kayla and Emily. When Jo Ann would tell us stories about their newest tricks or what they were saying or when they would come to the office with Kathy, the grandmother in her would take over and her normal effervescent personality would almost explode with pride and joy. She was equally involved with the rest of her extended family, her sister, and brothers. She talked about the cabin in upper New York and the holiday dinners with everyone together, and she told us about the football pool, and the rib roasts, and beer, and the shared vacations.

One could just sense the affection and closeness that existed among the members of this family—her personal family. But what I didn't realize was that she had more than one family; she also had a close family of nurses and staff with whom she worked, and who she nurtured and supported as if they were members of her immediate family.

This past week, a mother brought her sick child to be seen, and after the exam was completed, she related to me how much Jo Ann meant to her. She went on to tell me that she had immigrated to the US from Europe, and after taking a job here and there, had taken a position as a tech at the hospital in labor and delivery. Jo Ann had noticed her abilities and encouraged her to go on with her schooling—which she did. But she found there were many obstacles in the way of working full-time and going to school. She was about to be terminated when it was suggested to her that she speak to Jo Ann, who was the Head of Maternal and Child Health. She said Jo Ann jumped right in and helped her with her scheduling so she could juggle job and school and continued to support her until she finished her education—and then she gave her a job. With tears in her eyes she said, "I would not be who I am had it not been for Jo Ann."

Another RN told me about starting as an LPN working for Jo Ann—who always appreciated ability. She said Jo Ann encouraged her, perhaps even pushed her a little into advancing her education. When financial issues became a problem, she helped her fill out scholarship applications, which she eventually received. And then, after her shift was over, she would sit with her and help her with her nursing homework. She arranged her work schedule so she could attend school, work full-time, and manage her family—a pretty good trick for both of them, and I must tell you that I heard similar stories from four other nurses this week. As you might imagine, the devotion of these women to Jo Ann knows no bounds. But there is more; when these nurses achieved their goals, finished their schooling, or passed their boards, there were always cards with beautiful sentiments, flowers, and gifts, which they treasure and brought in to show me.

There is also a family of doctors—particularly pediatricians and family physicians, but also specialists—with whom she was constantly interacting in the hospital and office. Those of you in the medical community, I am sure, would agree that the relationships between doctors and nurses can, at times, be ambivalent—even somewhat testy—which isn't unusual in any working place where people work closely together, are dependent on each others efforts, and where there is constant stress and pressure in the work they are doing. I can assure you that the pressures of caring for sick children are immense—they are not less because the children are smaller. In the thirty years that Jo Ann worked with the doctors in this community, I never heard anything but the highest praise for her. She nurtured and taught and supported us as she did every other staff member. One physician said the other day, "You know, even where on occasion when she had reason to chew me out," (and as she assumed positions of leadership she did that with all of us), even then he said, "I never resented her reprimand—she never made me feel small." That was Jo Ann's special skill in dealing with people; she could correct you without tearing you down. She never degraded anyone publicly or privately; instead, she challenged people to be better—to have more confidence in themselves to be the person she told you she knew you could be—and then you went out and did it.

Her special gift was knowing how to approach people. She recognized when she had to be stern or when someone's ego needed stroking—or perhaps even a massage—but she also knew when all a person needed was to have his or her hand gently held, quietly.

And finally, there is a family of children who she served and to whom she dedicated her entire professional life. She never stopped thinking about ways to improve the quality of life for children and their families. She was timeless in her efforts on their behalf. She made the Sager Pediatric unit at Newcomb into a fine, efficient center for the care of sick children, and she insisted that it be child-friendly in every aspect, from the ever-changing seasonal decorations to the people she hired. You couldn't work for Jo Ann unless you loved children and understood their special needs and went the extra step to meet them. When she brought the level of care in pediatrics to where she wanted it to be, she began to look for other ways to improve the lives of young people in our community. She and the director of nursing, Jeanne Anderson, developed the concept and wrote the grant applications for the OK (Our Kids) clinic in 1988. It grew from two nights a week with a volunteer staff into a full-service pediatric clinic with full-time doctors, nurse practitioner, and staff. It provided well child and sick care for the many children in Cumberland County who had no access to private physicians. It served thousands of children—it was all Jo Ann's, and the clinic received constant accolades from the State of New Jersey.

She then turned her attention to other pressing health needs in our area. Unfortunately, Cumberland County has had a very high rate of adolescent pregnancies. Jo Ann recognized the special needs of pregnant teens in continuing their education and at the same time learning how to become competent and caring mothers. She wrote the application for the grant for The Impact Program, which provides educational and medical help both pre- and postpartum for the young mothers and their newborn infants. It is an outstanding resource for this community and would not be here but for Jo Ann.

Jo Ann was so humble—she never boasted, so we all took for granted all of her accomplishments. I never thought about what was the driving force behind her monumental efforts until this week. On Wednesday night, when Tom, Kathy, and Steve returned from Baltimore, we visited them at their home. We talked for a while and then Tom brought out a stack of newspapers that friends and neighbors had saved for him. These were papers filled with news of the accident in the Inner Harbor and with stories of Jo Ann and Lisa. There were papers from Baltimore and Philadelphia and New York and, of course, the local newspapers. Tom pointed to the newspapers and said, "I know Jo Ann is up in heaven looking down on us with a big smile on her face." I was startled by that statement and asked him why he was so certain, and he said Jo Ann was never sure she was doing enough—she always felt that she could do more and could be better at her work and that people didn't always understand what she was trying to accomplish, so that they didn't fully appreciate her efforts, and that what she needed to know more than anything else was that she was making a difference in the lives of the people she worked with and the lives of the children who meant so much to her. He went on to say that, "I have to believe that she knows about all these wonderful articles in the newspapers and the tributes paid to her on the TV programs, and so finally she knows she is appreciated and she can be at peace."

Hearing these words, I began to think about what motivated Jo Ann, and it was then that I understood that she did to herself what she did to others—only more so. She constantly challenged herself to be a better person, to work harder, to make a difference, to help make this sick old world a better place than it was when she came into it. She did all of that and she did it so well.

Tom, your words also brought some comfort to me, which I thought I would pass on to all of you. Since you assured me that she was in Heaven smiling down on us, I have begun to picture her in more detail. I see her in her new abode, where she was able to con the administration of the Heavenly Hosts to supply her with a very large office. On the door it says "Jo Ann Pierce, Director of Children's Welfare and Happiness." I am led to believe there is no sickness in heaven. She has a huge desk, and it is piled high with charts and papers—some are already stacked on the floor and bulging out of her closet, just like the clinic. I'm not sure what issues she has to tackle. I really don't know whether there are malpractice lawyers or insurance companies in Heaven—but if so, she will deal with them. Of course nothing has changed—Lisa is at her side helping her, and Jo Ann has already had to ask St. Peter on several occasions to help her find her glasses, and she has sent the angels scurrying about to locate her keys to open her desk. So you see, Tom, your words have comforted me, and I thank you for that.

In closing, I had wanted to sum up the life of this memorable woman, but I found myself struggling to find the proper words— it's so difficult because her life was so full. Then, this week, I was shown a letter that Jo Ann had written, and I knew immediately that her thoughts and her words painted a much more accurate portrait than any words that I could find. This letter was written by Jo Ann in 1999 when the Newcomb Hospital became part of the South Jersey Hospital Systems and the pediatric clinic was folded into the CHCI, which was already in place. Jo Ann sent this letter to each and every member of her staff, and it was saved by one of the nurse practitioners who brought it to the office this week to share with our staff. Here are her words:

Dear Children's Center Staff,

It is difficult to put into words my sincere appreciation for all of the years of loyalty, friendship, and caring that each and every one of you have given. This is not only to our patients, Newcomb Medical Center, and one another, but also to me. Your efforts will be sadly missed.

You can all be very proud of the positive team you created, and know that it would be impossible to duplicate. I can honestly say you are all my pride and joy, and I will never forget the quality and quantity of your efforts.

"YOU HAVE MADE A DIFFERENCE"

My belief is that we receive from life, from every experience, and from one another, according to what we have given. All of you should be beautifully blessed.

Each of us has an opportunity to let these experiences we have had open new doors for sharing our expertise and caring with others. I am confident that each and every one of you will open the doors with the same determination and love that I have witnessed in these past few years.

I wish all of you the success and happiness that I know you deserve. You will always be in my prayers and thoughts, and although we are separating for now, I would hope that we will all stay close forever.

Love always,

Jo Ann

In my heart I have to believe that Jo Ann wrote this letter to each and everyone who is here today.

Dr. David B. Rosenberg

LISA'S EULOGY
Written by Karen Quackenbush and David Clurman
March 14, 2004

Being able to stand here and talk about our friend and co-worker, Lisa, is one of the hardest things that we have ever had to do. When we started to think about what to say and how to say it, we realized that there are so many people that have been touched by Lisa, and we wanted to include their feelings, thoughts, and memories. Lisa is not only NJIT, but also Siena, Stony Brook, her circle of friends, her boyfriend Karl, her family, and so much more.

Lisa's career in student affairs started over ten years ago. During this time, Lisa had an enormous impact on anyone she came in contact with. One of the things I remember most about her is how she had the ability to challenge students to follow their dreams and hearts in anything they do. The lasting impact that Lisa has on students and staff can be seen through her work in a variety of ways; such as the Residence Hall Association, the Leadership Certificate Program, the Volunteer Incentive Program, and College Bowl, just to name a select few. She became a mentor to numerous students and staff, many of whom are here today. Lisa treated everyone with the same level of respect, no matter who you were or what level position you held.

Her strong desire to promote leadership is exemplified in the Center for Student Leadership, which Lisa founded two years ago. The center is a space that provides resources and workshops for students to develop their leadership skills and abilities. To honor Lisa's memory, NJIT is naming this center the Lisa A. Pierce Center for Student Leadership. This center will continue to encourage students to get involved in their community and make a difference, something Lisa always strived to do.

Lisa was one of the first people I [Karen] met at NJIT. I can still remember the day I moved into the residence halls as an Area Coordinator in Cypress Hall. The welcome wagon (i.e., Lisa) came to my front door and cheerfully greeted me with a basket of goodies and a bottle of champagne, explaining that we would enjoy the champagne later. While this was a unique experience for me, I know she has done this numerous times with other colleagues to make them feel welcome, at ease, and at home.

What I didn't know at the time was that Lisa would become one of the most important people in my life. Over the years, my bond with Lisa became more than just someone I worked with but someone who I could talk to about anything. I know I am not alone in having that type of relationship with Lisa. What is so unique about her is that many people felt a close friendship with her. She always made you feel like you were the center of attention, as long as the world still revolved around her.

I can remember the day Lisa met her "CAB,"* Karl, and how excited she was. She was floating on "cloud nine," knowing she just found the man of her dreams. She would talk to everyone about Karl on a daily basis and talk with Karl at least every hour via phone, e-mail, or text message.

Karl, she really enjoyed your public displays of affection, especially the abundance of flowers you sent. She would proudly display them for all to see and inquire who they were from. You meant so much to her, Karl, that she even curtailed her flirting. Lisa also had a strong bond with your son, Tristan. She spoke often of the care and admiration she had for him. Karl, you were her true love.

Family and friends were also very important to Lisa. She often spoke of her yearly trips to the Balloon Festival, camping, Saratoga race track, and the infamous Super Bowl party. Just like her students, she challenged her friends and family to accomplish their goals and grow beyond their comfort zone.

Lisa's parents were her strength and energy. If you ask people who knew them both, many would say that Lisa was very much like her Dad, smiling and always making sure you were happy. Her mother was a giving and caring person, both traits that Lisa had in abundance.

Lisa's nieces, Kayla and Emily, were the most important people in her life. When Kayla was born, she boasted to anyone who would listen that her baby was here. It was as if she just gave birth herself. Then, to really make her love affair complete, along came Emily. She was overjoyed at the fact that now her nieces could have the same relationship that her and her sister, Kathy, shared. Kathy and Lisa had a special bond that most of us can only dream of having. Lisa would speak to Kathy almost every morning, which helped start her day with a smile.

Lisa often had a smile on her face, even though it was sometimes caused by a mischievous thought. Lisa had two time zones: the coffee time zone, and the margarita and red wine time zone. In the morning, you could always expect Lisa to walk into work with a Dunkin Donuts coffee cup in one hand and her cell phone in the other, half asleep regardless of the fact that it was 10:00 a.m. In the other time zone, Lisa would send e-mails to all, inviting them to Happy Hour in the city somewhere watching her favorite band while enjoying a cocktail. Lisa would often drag anyone who would go to see her favorite new band, giving her the title "Groupie." We later found out she had a hidden agenda to make these bands famous, and her their manager. And who doesn't remember Lisa's cars? You could be getting ready to go out and complain you had nothing to wear. Lisa would run outside and come back in with a black skirt, in just your size, for the evening. Little did I know that very skirt was living in her car for who knows how long. You could also be serving dinner and make a comment about not having anything to drink with the meal. The next minute, a bottle of red wine would be sitting on your table, from where else but the trunk of Lisa's car. Lisa's car had many uses; her rear view mirror became her vanity to apply make-up and her butane curling iron to fix her hair on many occasions.

She had a competitive nature that was showcased in her card-playing abilities. Her favorite game, hearts, was a game she would play with many of the people here today. What is ironic is that she was playing a game that typified her nature.

Several years ago, Lisa decided to leave NJIT for another position. Before Lisa left, she made cards for all of her colleagues and friends, on the back of which was the following poem which summarizes what Lisa is all about:

Much of what we grow toward and change within ourselves has to do with what we respond to in others, what we learn from others, and what we understand about ourselves from others. Every time that you and I have been together, no matter how briefly, we've learned something—and that knowledge has become an important part of each of us, whether we are aware of it or not. So because of this, both of us have grown to be different persons than before we knew each other; and the persons we will grow to become, with or without the other by our side, will have gotten there partly because of our friendship. I don't know whether we'll spend more time together in the years ahead or merely drift apart, but I do know that since we have already touched each other and affected each other's life in some way, we can never be totally removed from each other's thoughts. I will always be part of you and you will always be part of me.

It is very difficult to share how much Lisa was loved and appreciated by so many different people. Know that she will live on in our hearts and our memories and never be forgotten. Lisa has affected us all and our future actions will continue to emulate her. Our lives have been forever changed because of her.

I know Lisa is sitting with us now, clapping her hands, smiling, and saying, "They love me, they really love me!"

Karen Quackenbush
And
David Clurman

* "CAB" = Cute-Assed Boyfriend

MY MEMORIES OF LISA
Written by Jane Roesner Graves
March 13, 2004

The last few days I've paid close attention to all the things in my life that remind me of Lisa. She's all around me. The day she died, a little bird came into our yard, singing the cheeriest little notes, hopping from tree to tree, investigating our bird-house and lighting up our yard. It was brownish grey with a coral/peach breast and head. Of course it made me think of Lisa, so lively and happy and curious. I think it may have been God's way of helping me remember the life about Lisa in a time when I was consumed with her death.

I'll miss my best friend. She was thirty-five. Her eyes were brown. She was the older sister. The newspapers tried to encapsulate her life, and they got some facts wrong, but as one friend said, "They also said she was full of life and an inspiration to others. They got that right." Yes, they did.

I keep remembering all the things I loved about her—her generous friendship, her laugh, her spirit, her vitality. She accepted others the way they were. I think that was her best quality. She assumed the best about people and made them feel that they were special, because she truly believed it. There are hundreds of people who consider Lisa their friend because of that unique ability to connect quickly and significantly with others. She made a difference in people's lives.

But Lisa was human and had some traits that, while lovable, could be annoying to a planner like me. We'd be on a road trip, or walking down the streets of New York City, and I'd ask, "So, you know where we're going?" "Yes," she'd answer with such confidence I'd believe her. We'd travel miles on the road or blocks in the city in the wrong direction before I'd inquire about stopping and looking at a map. "You have a map don't you?" I'd ask. "Yes," she'd answer with the same confidence as we barreled down some highway. "Where is that map?" I'd finally ask when we were completely lost, still speeding down the interstate. "In my trunk," she'd say.

Her car trunk. She would sometimes "pack" for a trip by throwing anything and everything she might need in the trunk of her car. It wasn't folded, it wasn't organized in any fashion I could make sense of, and her suitcase, when forced by airlines not to pack via automobile trunk, would be ridiculously heavy. Of course, it was "packed" in the same fashion as the car trunk, only in a smaller space. But it worked for her. Somehow, she had what she needed and could find it easily. And she always looked good with no evidence of car-trunk-rumple, as you would expect.

She loved looking good. One New Year's Eve, we walked through Worcester for First Night in sub-zero weather. She wore heeled boots, thin jeans, and a little coat while I put tights on under my jeans, wore my hat, gloves, earmuffs, and a bulky sweater. She looked great; I was warm. The next year's New Year's Eve, when we walked in Boston's sub-zero weather, she looked great again. I was warm again. One of the articles about the accident had a quote from a witness saying he saw a woman on a stretcher wearing only a thin top. "She wasn't dressed for the weather at all," he said. That's our Lisa. She always looked great.

Lisa was outgoing and fun and loving and a light; she was everyone's friend. But she was quiet and private about things that really mattered. I was blessed that she shared that side of herself with me, and I was privileged to meet those who were the most important in her life—her family.

She loved her mom and dad and sister, brother-in-law, her cousins, her uncles, aunts, and nieces completely without reserve. Football parties, Christmases, birthdays, Valentine's, funerals, vacations. Whatever the occasion, they supported and loved one another. She talked of the fun times they had and the fights they had. But the fights weren't a big deal, because they loved. It was just part of life and human nature. Lisa was great because her family is great. Lisa had her number one, most important support system in her family. We sometimes talked about how sad it was when we would hear colleagues tell us that we were their family, because we knew what they were missing. You guys are the best—never doubt how important you were in her life. Tom, you were her daddy. Kathy, you were her baby sister, no matter how old you got.

And oh, how she loved to talk about Kayla and Emily, her nieces, her "babies." It was such fun to hear how they were growing and changing. She was so proud of them and took such pleasure from their uncomplicated, complete love for her.

I didn't meet Karl before Lisa died. She loved him. She knew he loved her. I'm so happy she finally found someone who cherished her the way she deserved. She was finally complete. The last time we spoke, we talked about how she was saving for a house and her future together with Karl. I'm angry at fate and God and the powers that be that I have to meet Karl at her funeral instead of her wedding.

But I thank God for giving me my memories of Lisa. I cherish our spur of the moment Dunkin Donuts coffee runs. I can laugh at how she handled her cash (bills and change would be tucked into jeans, scattered through her trunk, loose in her purse. Was there any system there?) I treasure our memories of trips to Boston, Chicago, her trips to Kansas. Corn mazes, haunted houses, live bands, meals on her "Lisa" china, wine, tortellini, going to the grocery store at midnight, Guiding Light, mass on weekends, women's issues, eye-reading, advice on men, jobs, bosses, life. She did not "go gently into that good night." But I know God welcomed her with open arms because she was a soldier for Him. She made the world a better place while she was here, and her impact will be for always.

I love you, my dear Lisa. Thank you for loving me back.

Jane Rosener Graves

Chapter 1
The Preparation

Dear Reader,

The events of the past nine months have driven me to write many letters and speeches, and to tell many stories—stories about the accident, stories about the girls, stories about myself, but mostly stories about the things that have occurred since the accident.

Many of the people with whom I've shared these stories have told me that I should write them down. So, I felt compelled to write this book—sharing with you what I can only describe as the most phenomenal period in my life.

It seemed very appropriate that it took me nine months to give birth to this book. I suppose that is because I am hoping this book will live on for many years as a tribute to my wife, Jo Ann, and our daughter Lisa, and to prompt all of you to make a difference in this world.

I know that in this life Jo Ann and Lisa never felt they made a big difference, but they were wrong. They spent their lives trying to be the best they could be as individuals, and in doing so, touched the lives of everyone they met. They each spent their days making very small but meaningful differences in the lives of those they came in contact with. Differences that, in most cases, they never realized they made. Differences that may not have been shared with the world if they had died in a more timely or less tragic manner. Differences that may have been small in stature, but were enormous in quantity, and in numbers there is strength. If each of you reading this book can find small ways to emulate their ideals, we can make an enormous difference in this world.

In order for you to understand some of my stories, I have to start by telling you a little bit about myself. My Dad was killed in World War II when I was eight months old, so I never got to know him. Throughout my entire life people have told me how much I am like him. We apparently have very similar personalities and enjoy many of the same activities, even activities that no one else in my family participated in.

When my father was killed, my grandparents moved in with my mother and me for a while. My mother told stories about how every night for weeks when we sat down for dinner, the door bell would ring. They could clearly see the front porch from the dining room table, and it was obvious no one was there.

One night my grandparents went out, and my mother and I went to visit my aunt. We arrived home first, and when she was putting me in my crib, I asked where my grandfather was. She told me they had gone out and would be home later. I then looked toward the doorway and said, "Oh, there's Grandpa now." She was afraid someone else was in the house and quickly looked at the doorway, but no one was there. She looked back at me, and I had a puzzled look on my face, as if to ask, "Where did he go?" She was always convinced that it was my dad looking after me. I have always felt that my dad has been looking out for me my entire life.

* * *

Three years ago, my mother died at the age of ninety. On five different occasions after her death, my granddaughter Kayla, who was one and a half at the time, looked into the next room, got a bright smile on her face, and said, "Nana." She would then look back at us, puzzled, as we all stared at her in quiet silence.

* * *

The night that my father-in-law, Bill Fitzgerald, died about fifteen years ago, I was having trouble getting to sleep. I kept seeing a spot of blue light flickering on the ceiling. I could not find anything in the room from which it could be reflected. Then I realized that I could still see it when I closed my eyes. I got up and decided to have a beer for Bill. I noticed a bottle of scotch on the counter as I opened the beer. No one in the house drank scotch except Bill, and he had been in the hospital for weeks, so I was very surprised that it was sitting out. I had a scotch and a beer for Bill and went back to bed. I could still see the blue light when I got back in bed. I began thinking about Bill. Finally I said, "Don't worry about Marge (his wife). I will make sure that we all take care of her." The light disappeared as soon as I said that. I slept soundly the rest of the night.

* * *

As you can probably tell, I have always believed in an afterlife, and that those who have gone before us have ways to communicate with us and look after us. The events of the past nine months have reinforced those beliefs a hundredfold.

Jo Ann also believed in an afterlife. The house she grew up in was built by her great-grandfather. He died from a fall down the cellar stairs. I have heard countless stories from those who slept on the top floor of that house, including Jo Ann, about how someone would wake them by touching their feet. Some of them reported seeing an older man standing at the foot of the bed when they awoke. There are several family members who will not sleep up there, but it never bothered Jo Ann. She would just assume he needed a few more prayers and would say them before she went back to sleep. The last time this happened to Jo Ann was two years after we were married. I was on a business trip in New York City, so Jo Ann decided to stay with her parents. She said someone grabbed her ankles and would not let go. It startled her so much she let out a scream as she awoke. Everyone in the house woke up and came running up the stairs to see what was wrong. Jo Ann told them, "It's okay. Someone just grabbed my ankles and it startled me." They all went back to bed.

When Jo Ann's parents first moved into that house, her great-grandmother had a Tiffany-style lamp hanging over the dining room table. Jo Ann's mother never liked it. She had it taken down and put in the attic. Jo Ann, however, liked it and fifteen years ago decided to hang it over our kitchen table. It was in perfect shape. It only needed rewiring and a new bulb. I also screwed in a small device that would allow us to turn the lamp off and on by just touching any of the metal parts. It worked really well until Jo Ann's mom passed away. Every so often it would just go nuts. Off, on, off, on, for no apparent reason. Sometimes it would get so bad I would have to unplug it for a while. Jo Ann would just say, "Mom's trying to tell us something." It has been over a year now since Jo Ann reunited with her mom. The lamp has functioned perfectly since then.

A year before the accident, Jo Ann and I were watching the news when they started talking about a man who had lost half his family in a train accident. I turned to Jo Ann and said, "I don't know how anyone could handle that kind of tragedy. Family is so important to us I just cannot imagine how I would respond to something like that."

I met thousands of people after the accident who I know had these same thoughts about me, and they all had no idea what words to say to me to express those feelings. My answer was the same to every one of them. There are no words that can begin to express your feelings; there are only warm, tight hugs and a few shared tears. I would never have believed the emotional strength that can come from even a single shared hug.

The other thing that helped get me through this was that both of these women prepared us for it. Several times in the months prior to the accident, Jo Ann said to me, "I feel like I am dying." The first time she said this I got upset and wanted to take her to the emergency room. She said, "No I am all right, I just feel like I am dying." She said the same thing to her sister Mary. Then she told Mary, "I am not going to be here much longer."

On three different occasions Jo Ann said to me, "I would have to go before you, because you would find someone else and go on with your life, and I could never do that." I would get upset and ask, "Why are we having this conversation?" The last time she did this, I could not get her to change the subject until I got mad and said, "Jo Ann, listen to yourself. I am sixty years old, overweight, and bald, and those are only the first three things that come to mind, and you're making it sound like I am going to have women lined up at the door waiting to go out with me. Do you know how ridiculous that sounds?"

A year before the accident, Jo Ann was reading the paper and saw an ad for men's suits. She said "You need a new suit and they are on sale. I think we should go shopping tomorrow and look at them." I hate to shop, but I really did need a new suit, so I agreed to go. I found a brown suit that I liked and it fit very well, so I told her I would buy it. She said, "Try this one on, too. It's the same size and I think it will fit just as well." I said, "No. It's black, and I don't like black suits. I wouldn't wear it." She said, "Try it on." So I tried it on and we bought both suits. The black suit hung in my closet until the day of the funeral.

Two months before the accident, Jo Ann came home from work and told me that she met with the insurance people and they wanted her to get more life insurance. She was concerned because they wanted to deduct the payments automatically from our checking account and she was not sure we could afford them.

I was not sure that we could afford the payments either, but I could not talk her out of purchasing the insurance.

I was thinking about all of these things in the hospital the day after the accident. I told my daughter Kathy that I was not surprised I was still here, or that Jo Ann was not, but that I was surprised Lisa had not made it. Kathy said, "No, Dad, one month ago Lisa called me early in the morning all upset. She told me Grandma had appeared to her in a dream and told her that she would be with her shortly." Then Lisa said, "When I go into school today, I am going to contact the legal services that we recommend to the students and pay the fee to get the forms to make out a will, and if anything happens to me, I want my car to go to Karl."

Karl, Lisa's boyfriend, told me that Lisa cried like a baby when she had to leave for Baltimore, but that once she got into the van she was back to her normal, effervescent self. He thought it was very strange because it was so out of character for her.

A group from NJIT were supposed to attend a weekend conference for female engineering students. Lisa was not supposed to be driving the students to the conference. The woman who was scheduled to drive the van had to attend her grandmother's funeral, so Lisa told her she would drive the van for her. Lisa called us and asked if we wanted to join her for a weekend at the Inner Harbor in Baltimore. It sounded like a fun weekend so we told her we would meet her there Friday night. We arrived late and stayed up until 2:00 a.m. talking. It was raining on Saturday morning, so we slept late and did not walk down to the Inner Harbor until noon. We decided to have lunch while we planned what we were going to do that day. Our table overlooked the Harbor and we could see the water taxis and the tall ship, the USS Constellation. Jo Ann said she would like to take the water taxi to the different areas of the Harbor, and I told Lisa a story about the tall ship.

Lisa was born in Maryland while I was stationed at Edgewood Arsenal. Jo Ann's parents visited the weekend that Lisa was born and Jo Ann's dad wanted to see the ship. So, on Friday night we drove to Baltimore so he could see it. It had recently arrived at the harbor. There was no nice, safe, clean Inner Harbor back then. It was still a dark, dirty, scary waterfront, and Jo Ann told me that I could slow down to let Bill see it, but I was not to stop the car in that neighborhood. We drove by and then went home and had pizza and beer. Jo Ann went into labor at 12:30 that night. This is the first of what I refer to as my full-circle stories. I just found it fascinating that Lisa's life started and ended at the same tall ship. Coincidentally, the Living Classrooms Foundation, which owned the water taxi, also operates the tourist services on the ship for the city.

CHAPTER 2
THE ACCIDENT

We boarded the first water taxi after lunch for a trip to Fells Point. They told us during the trip that we could take a second water taxi from Fells Point if we wanted to see Fort McHenry. I thought the girls would want to shop in Fells Point, but to my surprise they both wanted to see the Fort. We boarded the last taxi to the Fort at two o'clock and spent two hours touring Fort McHenry.

Unlike the morning, which was cloudy and rainy, the afternoon was bright and sunny, but a bit breezy. The last taxi back to Fells Point was at 4:00 p.m.

The taxi was a glass-enclosed pontoon boat with only one door in the front. It was starting to cloud up as we got on the taxi. The captain was on the radio telling someone that there were more people who wanted to go back to Fells Point, but he already had a full boat. He told them he would leave a few minutes early and then come back for the rest of them.

As we pulled out over the Harbor, I could see a large black cloud coming over the buildings and out over the water. The water started to get rough and the rain started hitting the windows of the boat. I told Jo Ann that the storm wouldn't last long because it was bright and sunny behind the cloud. As soon as I said that, the wind started blowing the taxi around, and the first mate jumped up and stood in the center of the boat across from me. He asked everyone on our side of the boat to lean toward him. He then told the captain not to try to steer, just let the wind blow the boat the way it wanted. He then told us that they were trying to get behind a bulkhead to wait out the storm. I thought, "We are not going to get to any bulkhead; we are out in the center." Then, a second gust of wind hit the boat, and he asked everyone on our side of the boat to come over to his side. I was already on the edge of my seat leaning forward, so I jumped up as soon as he said that. I never saw anyone else on my side of the boat move. I just felt a third gust of wind hit the boat and watched the first mate's feet go out from under him, and he slid past me to my side of the boat. I looked back and saw everyone on the other side of the boat slide off their seats and across the floor to my side of the boat. The boat instantly flipped upside down. This happened just as fast as you are reading about it.

I now found myself with my head against the floor of the boat, which was now the ceiling. There was about a foot of air space on my left. It was only there for about two seconds. I did not see anyone else above the water, and once the air was gone you could not see anything in the water. I could not see or feel anyone around me in the water. My only thought was, "This is the day that the three of us go together." I said my last prayer and thought I would run out of air and be gone in seconds. But I was not out of breath yet, and I could not figure out why. It was a very pleasant and peaceful feeling, thinking that it was my last day on this earth. I would never have expected it to feel that way, but I will explain that later.

My right hand hit the life preservers that were stacked under the seats, and I realized that I did not want one of those. I had to get down to where the windows were so I could try to get out one of them. I pushed myself down and suddenly got caught in a strong current that sucked me through a window that someone had broken open. I could see light on the top of the water when I looked up. I kicked up, hoping I would get there before I passed out. I broke the surface and gasped for air and felt someone grab my shoulder and pull me over to the pontoon of the boat. He asked me if I was okay. I said, "Yes." He said, "Move down to the end of the boat and come around to the center where there is no pontoon and climb up on the boat and look for other people." I did that, but I never saw anyone emerge from the water after I did.

Once I was on the top of the boat I heard some of the women crying and someone was saying "Try to get someone's attention. Try using your cell phones." My cell phone was gone, and no one else's was working, but I looked up and could already see the Navy reservist boat heading for us. The reservist's first efforts were to try to secure the taxi to the side of the ramp of their boat so they could get us off the bottom of the boat. As soon as they realized that some people were still trapped inside the taxi, many of them dove into the water to try to save them. One of them almost got crushed between the two boats as they tried to pull them together. When they secured the taxi, they proceeded to help everyone off the bottom of the taxi and onto their boat. Once on the boat, I watched as they continued to try to save those still trapped underneath. Then they performed CPR and first aid on those they had already rescued. That group of men is, without a doubt, the most amazing group of men I will ever meet in this lifetime.

I looked up at the wheelhouse when the rescue ship started back to shore, and over it there was the most beautiful double rainbow that I have ever seen. I thought, "How appropriate that it should be going over these men at this time." But then I turned away, thinking, "I cannot appreciate this now." I had not seen Jo Ann or Lisa come out of the water, and I was sure I had lost both of them. I walked over to the side of the boat and stood shivering next to a beautiful young lady and her fiancé. I asked if they were okay and she said, "Yes, how are you?" I said, "I am okay, but I think I just lost my wife and daughter." She just reached over and held my hand for the rest of the trip in.

The people on shore were just as amazing as those on the boat. Everyone I came in contact with during the next four days reached far above the highest goal of service excellence that I can imagine—it was truly unbelievable. I am originally from Philadelphia, but I will forever think of Baltimore as my City of Brotherly Love.

CHAPTER 3
THE AFTERMATH

They got me out of my wet clothes and onto a heated mattress as soon as I arrived at the hospital and started checking me out and warming me up. I found it hard to believe that having five beautiful nurses undressing me as quickly as possible was not an enjoyable experience. The doctor kept trying to get me to call a family member and let them know what happened. I kept putting her off because I wanted to know what had happened to Jo Ann and Lisa before I called. A nurse came in a short while later saying that the accident was all over CNN. I suddenly realized I had to make the call before my family heard about it on the news.

It was not until 9:30 that night that I found out Jo Ann had been rescued by one of the fire department boats and had gone to a different hospital, but had not survived. Lisa had been rescued by the reservists and given CPR on the boat I was on. When she started breathing on her own, they transferred her to a fire department boat to get her to the hospital as fast as possible. She was on life support in a third hospital. I made a second call to my daughter Kathy, and they immediately transferred me to the other hospital so I could be with Lisa.

The first morning in the hospital I was watching a nurse insert an IV when I heard someone say, "Well, they told me I would have no trouble recognizing you." When I looked up, I saw a fire department chaplain who looked a lot like me. Father Burgess and I talked for a long while that day. First about how Kathy and I where holding up, then about the accident, and finally about Jo Ann and Lisa. At one point he asked me how long Jo Ann and I had been married. I told him thirty-seven and a half years. After a long silence I turned back to him and said, "And I've never been unhappy." He thought for a moment and then said, "You are a very lucky man." I told him, "Yes, I am." I hope that as each of you continue to read this book it will become obvious to you that I still consider myself to be a very lucky man.

I told Father about the accident. I told him that, in spite of feeling like I was about to run out of breath in the next few seconds, it had not been scary or terrifying; it was very peaceful. I had been very content with the knowledge that it would be my last day on this earth. I would never have expected death to be a pleasant experience. I don't believe I will ever fear death; in fact, I will look forward to it. I am in no hurry to die, but I will never worry about it again. It is just very obvious to me that I am here for a purpose. I still have a mission to complete. Perhaps my mission is to complete this book. Perhaps it is something entirely different.

I went on to explain to Father Burgess that back in December, Tony Feola, a good friend of mine from college, called and asked if I would like to attend a weekend retreat with him in Malvern. I said, "Yes," and Tony was very surprised. He had invited many friends to join him on his annual retreat for years, and as you might expect, it is not always easy to talk someone into going on a religious retreat. I had to tell Tony another of my stories. My mother always told me that my dad went to Malvern every year before I was born. I was actually excited when Tony asked me to go with him. It wasn't because I wanted to make a religious retreat. It was because, even though it was sixty years later, I wanted one more thing to share with my dad. Driving up there that Friday I kept saying to myself, "This is going to be good for me. This is going to be good for me! This is going to be good for me?" But on the ride home all I could say was, "I cannot believe how good this was for me." Jo Ann, who knew me better than anyone, could not believe how emotional I was about that weekend. Even Tony told me, "I think you got more out of that one weekend than I got out of all thirty years I have been going." Back then even I did not truly understand how good that weekend was for me. I think I would have been a basket case under that water, thinking that I was about to die, if I had not made that retreat. This annual retreat has now become one of the most important and on-going events in my life.

This, however, was not Tony's only role in helping me through this ordeal. The same morning I met Father Burgess, I realized no one would have called Tony or any of my other college friends to let them know I was okay. I called him to tell him what had happened. While we were on the phone Tony said, "I am coming down to see you." I told him not to come because I already had good family support, and there really wasn't anything he could do. He said, "Okay." About an hour later he called back and said, "I will be there in two hours." I said, "I knew you would be."

When Tony arrived, we walked down to visit Lisa and then sat and talked. He told me that before he came to the hospital in Baltimore, he drove into Philadelphia, went to the Miraculous Medal shrine in Germantown, and picked up three Miraculous Medals: one for me, one for Kathy, and one for Lisa. I sat there in total amazement. Tony lives just outside of Philadelphia, near the Pennsylvania Turnpike, and had a clean shot to Baltimore on the interstates. I asked him why he drove all the way into the city to do that and he told me he didn't know. I asked him if he knew the story about my mom, and he said, "No, what story?" I proceeded to tell him that my mother had always made the Monday night novena at that same shrine with her girlfriends when she was young. When she received the telegram that my dad was missing-in-action, she went right to that church and prayed that he really was just missing and not dead. She looked up and saw tears running down the face of the statue of Mary, and she knew that he was gone. She has always been devoted to that place. He said, "I never heard that story." Then he added, "I did think it was strange that while I was buying them, one of the priests walked in and offered to bless them for me."

I was thinking about this on the morning of the viewing in upstate New York. I got upset when I finally realized that he only gave me three medals and told me specifically who they were to go to. So as soon as Kathy got up, I said to her, "It is so obvious to me that my mom dragged Tony down there to get these medals; shouldn't I give my medal to your mother today?" Kathy said, "No, Dad. Mom was already up there; she didn't need one." I could not find fault with her logic, nor did I want to.

Chapter 4
The Rainbows

When Karl arrived at the hospital, I told him about everything that had happened, and when I told him about the double rainbow, he got tears in his eyes and said, "Thank you for telling me that. You do know that in many cultures a rainbow is considered to be the gateway to heaven, don't you?" I didn't, but I certainly believe it now.

A friend of mine from Columbia, Maryland brought me a picture of that rainbow a few days later. He told me that his granddaughter was getting ready to play in her very first soccer game when the storm hit. They canceled the game, but it was over so quickly that the coach said, "Well, let's at least take a team picture." He'd spotted the rainbow and took a picture of it, too.

* * *

The accident occurred at 4:00 p.m. on Saturday. Lisa remained in a coma until she passed away around 11:00 p.m. on Monday. We had two funerals. One in our hometown of Vineland, New Jersey, and one in Jo Ann's hometown of Hudson Falls, New York. During the viewing in Vineland, I was telling everyone that I had only seen a rainbow that beautiful one other time in my life. It was when we were driving to Sister Bernadette's father's funeral in Cape May. Sister was one of Lisa and Kathy's teachers. I told my cousin Joan that. She said, "That's not true, Tom. You have a picture of me under a rainbow like that." I realized she was right.

It was taken outside of the motel in Fort Edward, New York the morning of my wedding, August 13, 1966.

* * *

Exactly one month after the accident, I was doing some work at Dr. Dave's office and one of the girls who worked for Jo Ann asked me if I had seen the beautiful double rainbow the day before. I told her I hadn't seen it, and she said she'd taken a picture of it for me. When I saw the picture, I realized that it was identical to the one that had appeared the day of the accident.

* * *

In August I had to go north to Hudson Falls for a going-away party for Jo Ann's cousin. I went up a day early so I would be there on August thirteenth. The thirteenth would have been our thirty-eighth wedding anniversary. After putting roses on the graves, I went to the hall to help her aunt and uncle set up for the party. While I was there, my nephew Michael called and said, "Uncle Tom, I want you to go outside right now. Look south. Happy anniversary." There was yet another beautiful rainbow. I took a picture of this one myself. While I was taking that picture, my phone rang. It was my daughter, Kathy. She was just getting off the Adirondack Northway and was about a half hour away. She wanted to know if I could see the rainbow from where I was.

* * *

I went up to Hudson Falls again for Thanksgiving. I went up a day early so I could help my sister-in-law, Mary, cook dinner. Kathy could not leave until Thursday morning. When they arrived, her husband, Steve, said that she'd had a hard time that morning. He could hear her crying in the shower. I told him I would sit and talk to her, but he said, "No, she's okay now. She saw a beautiful rainbow while driving up the New York Thruway and watched it for about a half hour."

I find it hard to believe that these rainbows appeared at such significantly meaningful times, but it has been a very comforting experience.

Chapter 5
The "Thirteen" Stories

The first viewing in Vineland was on March fourteenth. The night before, almost forty family members and friends gathered at my daughter's to prepare ourselves for the days ahead. Many years ago I bought Jo Ann a very expensive bottle of very old Grand Marnier as a Christmas present. She couldn't believe I'd spent that much on one bottle, so she decided we would only drink it on very special occasions, like graduations, weddings, and births. Most of the time we would forget about it until well after the special occasion. I decided that this was the time to toast my girls. I started the toast by saying, "Today is the thirteenth. Jo Ann and I were married on August 13, 1966. Tomorrow at the funeral you will see a single yellow rose between the caskets, a rose that I am going to call the last rose, and I want to explain why it is there. One month after we were married, I bought Jo Ann a single yellow rose. She liked that. The next month, I went back to the florist and thought maybe I should buy her two roses. Then I thought, 'Nah, that could get expensive.' I bought her one rose. I bought Jo Ann a rose every thirteenth for thirty-seven and a half years." I wish I could remember everything else I said that night, but I can't. But the story of the roses is one that I have told hundreds and hundreds of times over the past nine months.

When most people hear the story they think how difficult that must have been, but it was never difficult. It was easy. It was fun, and it made every thirteenth a special occasion. It still does. It is something that I have recommended to many people over the years, but I don't know anyone else that has done it. If any of you want to try it, I will tell you the secret of my success. Always keep one or two special roses hidden away, like a silk rose, or a ceramic rose, just in case the stores close before you realize it's the thirteenth (or whatever your special date is). I promise you will never regret it.

* * *

When I went to the retreat this year, Father O'Donnell, the head of the retreat house, asked me to sit and talk to three other men in the group who had also lost loved ones in tragic accidents that year. The four of us spent over three hours discussing how we were dealing with it. One of the men, who lost his son, had many stories similar to mine. His son was always proud of the fact that he was the fifth generation with the same name. Instead of the number thirteen popping up over and over, his initials kept showing up. He hadn't been aware that his son liked to sing. While they were cleaning out his dorm room, someone gave them a picture of him singing at a karaoke bar. They said he loved to do that. When they looked at the picture they noticed that they could see the words he was singing on the screen behind him…"Only the good die young."

* * *

Each weekend retreat group has a name. The group I joined was formed back in the 1940s and is called The Lady of Fatima group. Our Lady of Fatima appeared to three young girls in Portugal for six consecutive months in 1917. She always appeared to them on the thirteenth!

* * *

In the first couple of weeks after the funeral, I was just not content with the rose between the caskets being the last rose. I decided that on April thirteenth I would send "thank you" roses to the people who had helped me through that first month. I went to my florist and asked him if he would help me to do that. He said yes, so I told him I would start giving him the names and addresses as soon as I could. I also told him that I wanted to send them anonymously without a card, just the way I gave them to Jo Ann. I knew that 90 percent of the people would know immediately who it was from as soon as they saw it and realized that it was the thirteenth. The other 10 percent I did not want to know my name. For example, I sent roses to the editor of the *Baltimore Sun*, and the editor of the *Vineland Daily Journal*. Neither I, nor any of my family, ever saw a reporter from these papers, yet they both printed the most beautiful stories about the girls that I could have ever hoped for. They did not approach me then, and I did not feel the need to give them my name now.

I was having trouble getting one address that I needed, and I had to get it to the florist in time for him to enter it into the computer by noon on the thirteenth in order to have it delivered that day. I finally got the address at 10:00 a.m. and rushed to the florist with it. When I got there, the florist said, "Come in the back, Tom, I have to tell you something." He was laughing when he said it, and I had no idea what to expect. He told me, "I just got off the phone with the FBI. Because you are sending all these flowers anonymously, they are checking you out as a terrorist threat. I had to explain to them who you were and why you are doing it." This is just one of my "thirteen" stories, but it is one of my favorites.

* * *

The rest of the stories started on the second day of the viewing in Vineland. There were so many people that they moved the viewing to the church so they would not have to move everyone to the church later for the Mass. When it came time for the Mass, the funeral directors had the pallbearers remove all the pictures and flowers. Then, they lined them up across the front of the church so no one could watch as they closed the caskets. I leaned over to Kathy and said, "I think that is just beautiful. It's like a wall of honor." Kathy looked at me in surprise and said, "Didn't you have anything to do with this?" I said, "No, why?" "You didn't have anything to do with this?" I again said, "No, what are you talking about?" She said, "Count the men up there." There were thirteen pallbearers.

* * *

Since the burials were going to be in upstate New York, we planned a luncheon in Vineland after the Mass. After talking to everyone, Jo Ann's cousin, Diane, realized that there were people there from thirteen different states.

* * *

Kathy and I had over thirty relatives staying with us from New York. We were all going to travel together the next day for the services up North. We got a phone call that evening saying that they were going to get twelve inches of snow the next day, and we would not be able to travel. I told everyone they would have to leave that night, and Kathy and I would wait and come up on Wednesday. While they were packing, my niece Nicole said to me, "Uncle Tom, can I have the roses from this one basket? I really love the color." I said, "Certainly." When she got home that night, she put them in a vase on the dining room table and counted them. There were thirteen roses. Her mom, Tina, had taped up the sympathy cards they received in the archways, the way many people put up their Christmas cards. She turned and counted them. There were thirteen on the left side, thirteen on the right side of the dining room, and thirteen on the living room doorway. Aunt Jeannette said, "Oh, I did the same thing." She then went around the corner to her house, and yes, she had thirteen cards hanging up.

* * *

When I was getting ready to send thank you letters and roses, I called Father Burgess in Baltimore to see if he could help me with some of the addresses. He was not in when I called so I wound up talking to his choir master. I gave him a list of the addresses I wanted Father to get for me and we talked for quite a while. I told him many of the stories I am telling you, and before we hung up he said, "I would like to tell you a story. When I answered the phone, I would have sworn that you were my brother in Oregon. You sound exactly like him on the phone. I cannot tell your voices apart, and his birthday is August thirteenth."

* * *

I have a cousin Sarah on my side of the family, and a niece Shawn on Jo Ann's side of the family and both had due dates of August 13, 2004. One delivered early and one delivered late.

* * *

Jane was one of Lisa's very best friends and her "Memories of Lisa" was dated March thirteenth.

* * *

My nephew Jeremy is a teacher in Glens Falls, NY. A few weeks after the accident, he called me and told me that they installed a new computer system at school that day, and all of the teachers had to sign-on and give themselves a username. The computer automatically assigned each of them a password. Most of them were something like 45G62. His came back as 13.

* * *

My daughter Kathy teaches sixth grade in Vineland. The day she went back to school, one of her little girls came up to her at the end of the day and asked, "Mrs. Cejkovsky, where have you been for thirteen days?"

* * *

At Easter time, I rode to upstate New York with Kathy and Steve. My watch and Steve's both beeped on the hour. Every time they went off, Kathy's car clock was exactly thirteen minutes fast.

* * *

When I went to the Adirondack Balloon Festival, I took over ninety pictures. When I got home I printed about ten of the best ones to show people. Each balloon at the festival has a small registration number that they have to hang on their basket. A few days later, someone noticed that one of my pictures was of balloon number thirteen.

* * *

Andrew Roccella was one of the other five victims of the accident. When I met his parents several months after the accident, his mom told me that Andrew was always into sports. He played football, baseball, and soccer. In every sport he played, he wore jersey number thirteen.

* * *

When I was making the funeral arrangements, the funeral director suggested I hire a law firm to help me through this. I knew that he had gone through a similar tragedy in his life, so I asked him whom he would recommend. I knew three of the four partners in the firm he suggested, so I called them that same afternoon. The only one in the office at that time was the partner that I did not know. He told me I did not need to do anything until after all the services were over, but that maybe we should meet and discuss what happened. As soon as I met him, I knew that I had to tell him another of my stories.

When you pick a firm to do work for you, you always wonder if you made the right decision. A few years ago, Jo Ann and I were at Mass and noticed a very attractive man about Lisa's age. Jo Ann asked me after Mass if I knew who he was. I did not, so she said we had to find out who he was and introduce him to Lisa. A few months later, Lisa was home for the weekend and went to Mass with us. She spotted him in church. Later, she asked if it was the same guy we'd told her about. We said he was. She said, "Oh my God, he could be a movie star. He could be a male model. Can you find out who he is?" He wasn't a movie star, or a male model. He was my new attorney. I had to tell him that it was very obvious I'd picked the right law firm for my daughter.

* * *

The second time I went to the attorney's office, I was waiting in the lobby reading the plaques on the walls when I realized that there were four partners in the firm but there were thirteen attorneys.

* * *

My attorney in Vineland referred me to a law office in Baltimore because the accident happened in Maryland. The first time I went to meet the attorney in Baltimore, I was again wondering if I had made the right choice. As I approached their building I noticed a small coffee shop on the first floor called the Daily Grind. I had no idea that the Daily Grind was a chain of coffee shops. I only knew of the one in Albany, which was Lisa's favorite place to go for coffee when she lived there. I suddenly felt much more comfortable with my choice. The lawsuit that they filed for me was dated May thirteenth.

* * *

When I left the law office that day I decided to have dinner before I drove back to New Jersey. There was a sports bar on the first floor right next to the Daily Grind with a sign that said "38 beers on tap." I thought, "I could use a beer," and decided to eat there. When I went in and sat at the bar, they gave me a list of all thirty-eight beers and all of the taps were lined up right in front of me. The first one on the list was Woodchuck Cider. It was Lisa's favorite. I hate it, so I chose another beer, and thought, "I'm sorry Lisa but I just can't do it." While I was having dinner someone ordered a Woodchuck Cider, and while the girl was filling the glass the keg kicked and blew the glass right out of her hand.

* * *

When I returned to Fort McHenry to speak to the firemen and families at the memorial service, they said the families could meet in the armory two hours before the service to get to know each other and prepare ourselves for the day.

Only a few of us took advantage of that opportunity, but as you might have expected, I told them some of my stories. Toward the end of the two hours, the fire chief came over and introduced himself. He said, "I would like you to meet my wife." He called her over and introduced me to her. He told her, "I want you to tell him what our special day is and why." She looked at him with a puzzled expression and then turned to me and said, "It's Friday the thirteenth. It's the day we met and he gave me a rose." The chief then looked at me and said, "I overheard your stories, so I had to let her tell you because I was afraid you wouldn't believe me."

* * *

When I first arrived back in Vineland after the accident, I had to start making the funeral arrangements. My brother-in-law George was like my guardian angel those first few days. He went everywhere with me. One morning we went out, and as we were about to get into the car, a woman pulled out of the driveway across the street and asked me how I was doing. She said if I needed her to cook, or clean, or talk, or if there was any way she could help, she was right across the street in the front apartment. I said thank you and she drove off. George just looked at me with an inquisitive expression. I said, "Don't look at me George, I never saw the woman before. I don't know if she's lived there two months or two years."

The day after the funeral services in Vineland was the first day I was totally alone. I pulled into my driveway around six o'clock that evening. I realized that the next day was trash day, so I started to drag the trash cans out to the front curb. When I looked across the street, my neighbor was also putting her trash out, and she walked across the street to talk to me. After a few minutes she said, "It's getting chilly out here. Why don't you come over and I'll make a couple of Manhattans and we can talk some more." I thought, "Well she picked the right drink for me, so why not?" We talked for almost two hours and we found that we had several mutual friends. I even knew her husband thirty years ago, before she met him.

About two months later I was talking to George on the phone and he asked me if I had seen any more of my neighbor. I said, "No," and he said, "I just thought I would check." My daughter teaches sixth grade at a school near my house. Some mornings she will stop in before school and put the coffee on if I am not up yet. The following morning was one of those mornings. She came in and started the coffee and called up to me. I told her I would be down as soon as I was finished getting dressed. She said, "It's getting late, Dad. I have to leave." I said, "Okay," and heard her leave and lock the door. A minute later, I heard her unlock the door and come back in. I called down, "What's wrong, Kath?" She said that my neighbor needed some help. I asked which neighbor, and she said, "The woman across the street, the blonde; she locked herself out and asked me if we had a ladder. I am going to take this little folding one over to her, then I have to leave." I said, "Okay. Tell her I will be over as soon as I am ready."

When I went over, my neighbor was walking around from the back of the house carrying the ladder. She told me that the only window that was unlocked was her bedroom window in the front of the house. I put the ladder under that window, raised the window and blinds, climbed into her bedroom, and walked through her apartment and opened the front door. She thanked me, and I picked up my ladder and returned home. The whole time I was doing this I was chuckling to myself because I have only climbed into a woman's bedroom window one other time in my life. It was on my wedding day. When Jo Ann and I left the reception, we had to go back to her house to get our luggage. My mother-in-law was supposed to give us a key, but of course, we forgot to get it. I had to get a ladder out of the garage and climb into my mother-in-law's bedroom window. It was definitely déjà vu. As I continued to get ready for work, I burst out laughing when I suddenly realized that it was the thirteenth. I had to call George to tell him the story.

Chapter 6
The Other Stories

A month before this happened I received an e-mail from Meg, who I refer to as "my third daughter." When we first moved into our house in Vineland thirty-two years ago, Meg was a little girl who lived one house down from us. She was one year older than Lisa and pretty much lived at our house for many years. Two months after we moved into the house, Meg's dad was killed. Meg was only five at the time, and she had two older brothers who never dealt with his death well. Her e-mail was to tell me that her oldest brother, Bill, was not doing well. Someone had borrowed his car and totaled it, so he was having a hard time getting to work. He was losing his job and his apartment. This was not something I wanted to deal with, but Meg had flown in from Arizona to be with me after the accident, and I could not ignore her problems now. A week later I had a new roommate. I felt that this would be a total disaster for me, but Bill and I got along very well. He obviously needed my help, and he showed up at a time in my life when I really needed someone to talk to. The first night we stayed up until 1:00 a.m. talking. It was during this conversation that I realized we were a match made in heaven. His dad was killed thirty-two years, to the day, before the accident. Both occurred on March sixth.

The only thing my neighbor said to me the day I crawled through her bedroom window, besides thank you, was that she was getting ready to move to Florida. She called me the next day and asked if she could take me to dinner for helping her. I said, "Yes," and asked her when she was moving to Florida, and how much her rent was. The amount she was paying was half of what I expected it to be, and I suddenly realized that my wife had dragged me through her window so I could help Bill move on with his life. Three weeks later, she moved south and Bill moved into his new apartment.

* * *

Two months after the accident my friend Matt called to see how I was doing. He told me that he was going to Tony LeStorti's house for dinner that night, and that he was going to ask Tony to sign a copy of his book. Tony is another of my college friends. I, of course, immediately asked, "What book?" Matt told me Tony had written a book and just had it published. He said it was called *When You're Asked to do the Impossible*. I told him I had to have a copy of that book, because I felt like I was doing the impossible. Matt ordered me a copy from Amazon. com and I started reading it as soon as it arrived. The book starts out by talking about Roger's Rules for Rangers written in the 1800s and how they are still the foundation of all ranger-type programs throughout the world. These rules were written on Roger's Island in Fort Edward, New York. The island was Roger's base camp during the French and Indian War and is only ten minutes from where Jo Ann grew up. Two weeks prior to receiving it, I was up north and had visited the new Roger's Island Museum.

The rest of the book applies these rules to leadership development in business today. As I continued to read the book, there were times when I felt he was talking about me, and times when I felt like I was listening to Jo Ann talk about team development at the hospital. Then I finally realized that the book would have to be my first contribution to Lisa's new Leadership Development Library at NJIT.

A month later I met with Tony, and I had him sign a copy of his book for me. I also asked him to sign one for the students of NJIT in Lisa's name. As you might expect, I also told him many of my stories that day. At one point I told him that I had met the president of the Living Classrooms Foundation, Mr. James Bond, at the funeral. Then Tony told me he had a story to tell me. He told me that when he taught at Gwynedd-Mercy College, his office used to be James Bond's office. The James Bond he was referring to taught at the college prior to Tony's arrival. He said that Bond was an ornithologist and wrote several books about birds. When Ian Fleming began writing his first James Bond novel, he had a copy of one of Mr. Bond's books on his desk and had decided that would be a good name for his now-famous spy.

* * *

On the night that Lisa died one of her friends in Connecticut sat up in bed saying, "She's here, she's here." It woke up his wife, Kelli, and she looked at the clock. Brian then laid back down and went back to sleep. He does not remember doing it. The next day Kathy called Kelli to tell her that Lisa passed and Kelli asked her if it was around 10:45. The actual time was 10:47.

* * *

Many people have asked if I have dreamed about either Lisa or Jo Ann. I tell them that I have not. I do believe that Jo Ann has woken me up in the middle of the night on at least three different occasions to tell me something, and her message is always obvious to me at the time. She did, however, allow me to see her once. Jo Ann and I always worked strange hours, so we ate out more than most people. The day we arrived back in Vineland after the accident, I was sitting at the dining room table looking for the phone number of one of our favorite restaurants so I could arrange for a luncheon to follow the funeral. I'd lost my organizer in the Inner Harbor and was having a difficult time finding the number. Suddenly my phone rang, and it was the owner of the restaurant I was trying to call. I told her I was about to call her to arrange for the luncheon. She said she would take care of that for me and wanted to know how I was doing. I told her we had just gotten back from Baltimore and I was fine. She said, "I am bringing dinner over tonight." I said, "There are thirty-six of us here." She said, "That's okay. I will be there with dinner." When she arrived with dinner she was very emotional, so I sat down in the rocking chair in the living room and she sat on the ottoman. I told her about the accident and tried to calm her down. Between my conversation and the thirty-six people having dinner, the house was somewhat chaotic. The last thing I was thinking about was Jo Ann, but in the middle of my conversation I got the urge to lean forward in the rocking chair and looked toward the steps. Jo Ann was standing at the foot of the stairs, and I knew immediately what she was trying to tell me. I just smiled and thought, "Yes, I know. It's okay." And I sat back and continued my conversation.

* * *

On another night, while everyone was still in Vineland, we sent out for Chinese. I was sitting at the dining room table after dinner when my brother-in-law George said, "I think I will have dessert," as he reached for a fortune cookie. He read the fortune to himself and stuffed it into his fist. I could tell he did not want to share what it said. Then my nephew Michael grabbed a cookie and also read the fortune to himself. Then he handed it to me. I told the others, "This was obviously meant for me," and I read it out loud. It said, "You will live a long life." Then George handed me his fortune. It read, "You and your wife will have a happy life together." We all knew they were both meant for me.

Last week I stopped for Chinese food on my way home from

work. When I finished I found two fortune cookies in the bag. They read, "You are one of those people who goes places in life," and, "You will win success in whatever you adopt." The events of this year have certainly made me feel like both of these fortunes were also meant for me.

* * *

Shortly after Lisa's death I was approached by someone from the transplant center to ask if I would allow her organs and bones to be harvested for others. I said yes because I knew that Lisa would love knowing she was helping others. They said that her contributions would help over ninety different people. Just before the first anniversary of the accident, someone from the center called me to see how I was doing. She also told me that Lisa had helped a one-year-old boy in Atlanta and at least four other people with knee problems across the country. I cannot imagine a better way for her life to go on than that.

* * *

In order to help my own life go on, I decided I needed to lose weight, so I signed up at a local gym for the over-forty crowd. They let me join, even though I still think of myself as only being twenty-five. I was determined to make this a lasting commitment, so I joined for the entire year and even paid in advance. The therapist said, "Since you're doing that, we can add an additional month and give you a 10 percent discount. This is going to work out to be better for you than a baker's dozen."

* * *

My brother-in-law Mike has run a football pool for the last thirteen years and everyone in the family is in it. We all have nicknames in the pool. Since I am from Philly, my nickname has always been Bald Eagle. I don't remember what Lisa's nickname was in the beginning, but three years ago she changed it to

Dark Cloud. I never understood that name for her, but after the accident I had to find out why she picked it. My nephew Michael told me that before he started college, Lisa rounded him and his friends up to talk to them about what to expect when they got to college, what they should avoid, and what was really important. They told her that she was casting a Dark Cloud over their college life. I believe that nickname was her way of keeping her thoughts with them so they would stay focused throughout their college careers.

* * *

A few weeks ago, my nephew Jeremy called me. He said, "Uncle Tom, I have another Aunt Jo Ann story." I said, "I'm listening." He said, "You know that I have coached wrestling for several years now. Well, this year I was the head coach, and when you have a student in the finals, it is a tradition that the head coach wears a suit during the final match. We had an excellent team this year, and the state championships were last Saturday. So I had to have a suit. I had been searching for my suit coat ever since the school year started but had not found it. Last week, I went through every closet in the house. I looked in the cars. I looked in the cellar. I looked in the garage. I went to my mom's and searched. I called my friends and had them search. But I just couldn't find it. Friday night I told Shawn (his wife) that I would have to go buy a new suit first thing in the morning so I would have something to wear Saturday night. I really liked my old suit and didn't want to buy a new one. I sat forward on the couch before we went to bed and looked up and said 'Aunt Jo Ann, I need you to help me find my suit. The last time I wore it was when I read your eulogy at the funeral, and I really need it for tomorrow.' Shawn was laughing at me. I woke up with a start at 5:00 a.m. and told Shawn, 'It's under the basement stairs.' We went down and pulled out two plastic bins, an old sleeping bag, a comforter, and under all of that was my suit coat."

* * *

During the second funeral Mass in Hudson Falls, New York, the priest pointed out that it was the feast of St. Joseph, the patron of a happy death. When I heard this I couldn't help but think about how peaceful I felt under that water, thinking that it was my last day on this earth.

* * *

There have been many things that have made me feel peaceful this year. The week before the accident, Jo Ann let the washer fluid in her car run dry and the message "low washer fluid" would show up each time she started the car. I have filled that tank many times this year, but I have not been able to stop this message from appearing. It has been nice feeling, like she always travels with me.

CHAPTER 7
THE HEADLINES

I know that most people who do not know me well, or who have not seen me in a long time, have just assumed that I must be suffering a tremendous amount of grief and sorrow. If I were outside looking in at this, I know that I would share those feelings. But I have been in the center of this, surrounded by a cocoon of love that is just mind-boggling. Neither I nor anyone in my family has ever been approached by a reporter. In Baltimore I had a police officer by my side twenty-four hours a day. I knew I would not be bothered there. What I did not realize was, back in Vineland and at NJIT, we had an army of friends who were telling the most beautiful stories about Jo Ann and Lisa. All of these people allowed us to go through the process of mourning and saying good-bye in a completely quiet and private setting which was so very much appreciated by the entire family. At the same time they softened our sorrow by allowing us to share Jo Ann and Lisa's beautiful lives and accomplishments with the world.

While I was in the hospital I did not watch any TV or read any newspapers until Karl came running into my room saying, "You have to read the *Baltimore Sun*. You have to read the *Baltimore Sun*…" I said, "Calm down. Why do I have to read the *Baltimore Sun*?" He said, "Here," and put the paper in my hand. When I opened it to page two, I saw a picture of Jo Ann under a headline that read, "A Phenomenal Nurse who was Devoted to Kids," which was the first of many beautiful articles. I still cannot find words that would describe the emotions of that moment.

Jo Ann and I moved to Vineland just after Lisa was born. When I left the service I received a job offer there. Vineland has never been known as an overly friendly town. Anyone not born here is always considered an outsider. I would never have expected the overwhelming outpouring of love and admiration for those two that flooded the front pages of our local newspaper on more than eight different days.

The day before I arrived home the headlines were, "Baltimore tragedy hits home. Vineland health care worker dies in harbor mishap. Daughter critically injured on Pierce family trip." The story took up most of the front page and was continued on page two.

The next day, the center of the front page was a huge five-by-eight picture of Jo Ann with a headline that said, "Co-Workers reflect on victim's strength." To the left of the article was a small, one and a half inch picture of Martha Stewart. (I could not resist hanging this page up at the funeral with a sign saying, "She's bigger than Martha.")

The very next day the headline was, "Daughter succumbs to injuries," with another beautiful article about Lisa that ended with a story about both of them that came from a friend in Australia. Don't let anyone ever tell you that this is not a very small world.

The following day, both their pictures were on the front page announcing that their obituaries were on page four.

The day after the viewing the headline was, "Hundreds bid farewell to the Pierces," with yet another fantastic article. The next morning after the funeral Mass, we again took up almost half of the front page with headlines of, "…Two very special people. Funeral lauds lives of ferry victims."

At this point all I could say was, "*wow*," and both of Jo Ann's brothers were wondering if they ever really knew their sister. I can assure you they did. They just didn't realize how many other people knew her, just in a slightly different way.

The next morning, I was getting dressed when the phone rang. The voice on the other end said, "Tom, have you seen today's paper yet?" I said, "No, Murray, but I cannot imagine that there is anything else they could possibly find to say about them." He said, "Go get the paper," and hung up. The headline was, "I didn't know you but you changed my life." The story took up more that half of the front page and all of page seven. The top of page seven said, "Farewell, Lisa Pierce. You gave me the greatest gift I've ever received." It was Henry Zecher's letter to Lisa, which I have included below.

FOR LISA
By Henry Q Zecher
March 17, 2004

I didn't know you, but you changed my life. By all accounts, you were a very special person. You left a lasting impression on every one who came in contact with you. I was no exception.

We were brought together by chance; a trick of fate that no one could have foreseen. What started out as a typical day turned into a nightmare in an instant. It seems like a dream to me now— the wind...the cold...the rain...the frigid water...the cries of pain and panic...the desperation.

It was around 4 p.m. Things were winding down and we decided to take a short break before cleaning up. I sat drinking some iced tea and thumbing through an old issue of *All Hands*, the navy's official monthly publication. Jeff King and Greg Baccala were talking about motorcycles, I think. I remember Jeff saying, "Damn, brother! Look at that black cloud rolling in!" I looked up in curiosity. Outside the window, where a minute ago the sun was shining, was one of the darkest storm clouds I have ever seen.

The power lines outside the window began to gyrate wildly as the wind began to blow. Greg looked out the window at the harbor below. He turned to Jeff, "Hey man, there's whitecaps out there!"

Jeff was incredulous. "What? Man there ain't no whitecaps out there!"

"Come look," said Greg. They disappeared into the hallway and I returned to my article about career opportunities for military personnel separating from active duty. "I should have read this twelve years ago," I remember thinking.

A couple of minutes later, I heard shouting coming from down the hall. I looked over my shoulder as Greg ran in. "Zecher, a water taxi just flipped over! Come on, let's go!"

I followed him down the stairs and out the back door toward the boat dock. We boarded the old LCM-8 landing craft and pulled out every life jacket we could find. The LCM had made a name for itself during World War II. Designed for transporting personnel and cargo, it was utilized to carry soldiers to the beaches at Normandy during the D-Day invasion. The reserve center uses it for training exercises now. She's gotten temperamental in her old age and never fires up on the first try. But that day, with one turn of the key, she turned right over and the engines roared to life like a great lion in the wilds of Africa.

On the dock, some of our shipmates, who chose to stay behind to convert the drill hall into a make-shift triage, threw off the mooring lines. We backed away from the dock and turned to head toward the scene of the accident, roughly 1000 yards off.

The clouds were dark and hateful. The current churned and rolled as our boat pitched up and down, back and forth. I stood on the side of the boat, holding the rope that served as a guard rail, along with a handful of my shipmates; all of us focusing on the wreckage that lay before us. The wind beat against us and the rain pelted our bodies so hard it was painful. It felt like we were getting hit with thousands of small rocks.

Jeff jumped down and ran toward the wheelhouse, emptying his pockets and stripping off his camouflage blouse. "What a good idea," I thought. I followed and did the same.

"I'm emptying my pockets in case I have to go in, brother," he said to Senior Chief Scardina, who was piloting the boat.

"I hear ya," said the senior chief, turning his hat around backward to get a better view.

I think we were fifty yards away when I was finally able to get a clear view. Some were on top of the over-turned vessel. Others were in the water. The ones in the water were struggling to climb onto what was left of the boat.

"My God!"

"There are people underneath!" "My daughter is under there!" "Please help us!" The screams were unified, yet random and scattered.

The moment had arrived when I was faced with the appalling question, "Of what is my soul made?" I wanted to be brave. I wanted to be strong. I wanted to be heroic. The truth is I was terrified beyond the capacity for rational thought. I could only react. Split-second decisions had to be made. If you hesitate, people are going to die.

The first thing my eyes focused on was a frightened young girl who was crying hysterically and clinging to an adult next to her. My only thought was, "I've got to get to that child."

The strong current made it virtually impossible to get close enough. Senior Chief Scardina lowered the ramp and two men dove into the water to try to free those trapped underneath. After two failed attempts, they called back to us, "We can't get in." A third man dove in to assist. They disappeared under the water for what seemed like an eternity. Again, they surfaced, clearly frustrated and already starting to succumb to exposure to the 43-degree water.

"I can't find a door."

"The windows won't break out."

Precious seconds that could mean the difference between life and death were flying by.

Someone threw them a lifeline. "Tie it around the motor," one guy yelled. No one moved. "Tie the rope around the motor," I repeated. Again, no response.

I recalled a line from the album, *Jesus Christ Superstar,* "Why do you not speak when I have your life in my hands?"

We made circular motions with our hands, "TIE THE ROPE AROUND THE MOTOR SO WE CAN PULL YOU TO US!!!!" Finally, one man grabbed the rope and tied it to the motor, his nearly-frozen hands trembling.

Three or four men pulled the rope with all their strength.

The current pushed the boat toward us faster than we were able to control as we twisted and turned in the swirling water. Jerry Neblet, who was the first to enter the water, got caught between the two boats and was nearly crushed. At the last second, he managed to pull himself up and ended up on top of the overturned water taxi. Commander Decker, who was soaking wet, lost his footing and fell backward, hitting his head on the side of the hull. He passed out and went in and out of consciousness a number of times, his head bleeding profusely. "I'm okay," he kept saying. Then he would pass out again.

We reached out our hands to the soaked passengers and began helping them onto our deck. I kept my eyes focused on the young girl. Finally, I was able to reach out to her. Another passenger lifted her up and to me so I could get hold of her. She grabbed my hand and I wrapped my other arm around her waist.

"Come on, sweetheart. I've got you. You can do it."

I set her down and a shipmate wrapped a blanket around her. The adult she had been clinging to got on and she ran to him. They embraced. I breathed a sigh of relief and turned back toward the remaining passengers.

Some of my shipmates wrapped people in blankets. Others stripped off their jackets and put them over the shoulders of the shivering survivors.

"There are people underneath," they continued to yell.

As the last person got off the doomed vessel, our minds raced. How do we get to ones still trapped below?

Senior Chief yelled from the wheelhouse, "Move!! I can't see!"

Neblet dove in again to help Lieutenant Commander Eisenstein, who was treading water a few feet away, waiting for a chance to do something…anything. His eyes never left the taxi.

Senior Chief called for us to back away from the edge. "I'm gonna use the ramp to lift it up!" In retrospect, I'd say it was a stroke of genius.

The ramp wasn't designed for this, but it was the only chance we had to get to those still trapped inside. Improvise, adapt, and overcome. That's what they teach you in the military. That statement had always been kind of a cliché and a joke to me. But this was no cliché. And there would be no punch line.

The ramp lowered and two or three of us began to move back toward the edge. Chief Johnson and I glanced at one another and he nodded at me. No words were said. It wasn't necessary. Others moved up behind us. Jeff King moved to the other side of me.

The ramp caught hold of the boat and began lifting upward. My body stiffened as water rolled up onto the deck and came up to around our knees. I inhaled deeply and closed my eyes for a moment. I couldn't believe how cold it was. I looked down at Neblet and Lieutenant Commander Eisenstein in the water below us. How they withstood it for so long, I'll never know.

As the boat lifted into the air, debris began to float out from underneath: purses, clothing, paper, back packs. Within a few seconds three people floated out, face down. The first was a male, probably middle-aged. I still don't know his name. Lieutenant Commander Eisenstein grabbed him.

The second was Sarah Bentrem, the eight year-old girl. When I saw her, I immediately wanted to go in after her. Before I could even think about it, Jeff was already in the water. Lieutenant Commander Eisenstein grabbed for Sarah.

He said later, "I couldn't hold them both so I had to make a decision. I had to let one of them go." I can't imagine having to make a decision like that. How do you choose one life over another?

[We think the man was picked up by one of the Fire Department rescue boats. But no one is really sure.]

Jeff and the Commander turned Sarah's limp body over and the two of them tried to lift her up and out. The current bashed them mercilessly against the side of the boat. Eventually, they were able to get her to safety and two guys immediately began administering CPR. They worked feverishly to revive her.

You were the last to emerge from under the broken boat. The Chief saw you first, I think. Truthfully, I don't remember. He said, "I've got another one! I need help! I've got another one." He had hold of your shirt. You were still face-down. I reached down and grabbed your arm. Together we began to pull you up.

"Come on, sweetheart. I've got you. You can do it."

The first thing I saw was foam seeping out from your mouth and nose and your pale, blue skin. Your blonde hair was hanging straight down, partially obscuring your face. I remember that you were wearing a black blouse, black pants, and black boots.

My hands started to ache from the cold and your wet skin began to slip out of my grasp. "Oh God," I thought, "If I drop her, she's going to sink like a stone."

"No! Don't you fall on me! Please!"

I reached down with my other hand and tried to grab for your pant leg. Your water-logged body hung precariously in the air, half in and half out of the water. Chief Johnson called over his shoulder, "We need help!" I couldn't reach far enough without losing my grip on your arm. You slipped again and I started to go forward. My soaked boots gave me no traction. I was halfway off the ramp.

I said to Chief Johnson, "I'm losing her, Chief. I can't hold on."

Again, he called for help.

Jeff, who had been in the water all this time, tried to help by pushing you up to us. He had become entangled in the lifeline and had been repeatedly been smashed against the side of the boat by the wicked current. It was clear that he had nothing left. He looked up at Chief Johnson and, with an expression that conveyed both pain and guilt, said, "I'm so exhausted."

I struggled to regain my grip on your arm. My boot slipped and I started to stumble backward. I grabbed your hand. Your other hand still dangled just beneath the surface of the water. Your body turned toward me and your head rolled to the side so that I could clearly see your face looking up at me. Your eyes were still open. They were a pale blue color...not much different than the color of your skin. At that point I thought you were already dead

"Oh no. Please! A just and loving God wouldn't allow this to happen. Please!"

Then I looked into your eyes and time suddenly stood still. Something touched me down in the very depths of my being. For a fleeting moment that now seems like an eternity, I felt like I was looking right into your soul. "Don't let go," you seemed to be saying. "You can do it."

For some reason that I still don't quite understand, I started shouting at you; pleading with whatever will to live was left in you not to give up. I could feel tears welling up in my eyes and I almost cried.

"COME ON, BABY! COME ON! STAY WITH ME, BABY! KEEP FIGHTING! DON'T LEAVE ME!"

"Dammit," the chief yelled, "We need help!"

"COME ON, STAY WITH ME...."

Three other shipmates all grabbed onto you and we all pulled and finally got you into the boat. I fell backward onto the deck.

"Stay with me..."

Chief Johnson yelled, "CPR! Get ready! CPR! Get ready!"

Commander Decker, even in his haze, leapt forward and began breathing into your mouth as the chief performed the chest compressions. I backed away to give them room.

"Please..."

The other three, who helped pull you in, grabbed Jeff and pulled him into the boat. He got up after a few seconds and headed toward the wheelhouse. He was shaking uncontrollably.

I watched them perform CPR on you until the rescue boat

arrived. They handed over a stretcher and strapped you in. As the rescue boat pulled away, Commander Pender said, "She's breathing on her own."

Sarah, the young girl, was also put in a stretcher and taken away on a rescue boat.

At that moment, I looked up and saw that the rain had suddenly stopped. The sun shone brightly and there were two giant rainbows directly above our heads. It was as if we had been blessed.

"Thank you."

I walked back toward the wheelhouse to check on Jeff. He asked me to get him some rags from down below so he could dry off. After I gave him the rags, I turned and walked out to see what else needed to be done. I passed one of the men who had performed CPR on Sarah. He had tears in his eyes. I asked him if he was okay. "I've got two babies of my own," he said. "This ain't supposed to happen."

We turned and headed toward shore. Pat Elwood was standing on the side, holding the rope, and looking out at the scene of the accident. He pointed to where we started before drifting down toward the Key Bridge. (We had drifted a total of a quarter of a mile in the time since we arrived on the scene) There were objects still floating in the water. He couldn't tell if they were people or pieces of debris. He asked me if I could tell what it was. I couldn't make it out, either.

We yelled at one of the rescue boats, "Over there...go look over there."

We started going around to all the passengers to check on their condition. I went to one man, (who I later realized is the father of Corinne Schillings, the 26 year-old woman who is still missing) and asked him, "Are you okay? Is there anything you need?"

He said, "I need my daughter." He turned his head toward the water. "And she's still out there."

What do you say to a man who has just lost his child? How do you give comfort to someone in that position? I can go home and hug my daughter all night long. He'll never know that feeling again.

"I'm sorry," I said. Then I closed my eyes and walked away.

Our boat arrived at the pier and our shipmates came out to assist the victims. We off-loaded the victims and took them in to be treated. The rescue squad and EMT's were already there and began administering first aid.

Your mother was alive when we got there, but had to be carried off. I don't know for certain, but I don't think she went into cardiac arrest until after she had arrived at the hospital.

Another woman had a broken arm and broken collar bone. She screamed when they lifted her onto the stretcher. Others had bruises and contusions. Some were bleeding. All were in various stages of hypothermia. We got them coffee, tea, hot chocolate… anything we could find.

Some of the men who went out on the rescue boat were taken to Bethesda Naval Hospital to be treated for exposure and checked out to make sure they were okay. I changed out of my soaked clothes. As I was leaving, I passed Master Chief Johnson who had witnessed the accident from the bottom floor and called 911. "So, Master Chief," I asked. "Are you gonna come rock me to sleep tonight?"

"Buddy," he said, "I'm gonna bring you a beautiful woman and a bottle of Jack Daniels." We laughed, knowing that we both needed to desperately. He shook my hand and said "I'll see you in the morning."

"I'll be here with bells on," I said.

I waved to Senior Chief Scardina. He gave me a thumbs-up.

I climbed in my vehicle, put my head on the steering wheel, and cried.

The next day, the Reserve Center was a media circus. We did our best to explain what we had seen and experienced. Each man gave his own perspective on the events. I spent a good deal of time talking with David Snyder of the *Washington Post,* who wrote a wonderful article about it. It was even on the front page. He asked if I would be willing to meet you once you had recovered. I told him that I thought you needed some time with your loved ones, but that if you would have me, I would be honored.

The phone calls came fast and furious on Monday, after the article hit the newsstands. I told everyone that, as far as I knew, you were doing okay and still fighting the good fight.

I did my best to collect as much information as I could about your condition and that of Sarah Bentrem. I prayed for you every day.

"Stay with me. Keep fighting…"

I finally learned your name on the afternoon of Tuesday, March 10.

Later that day, just after 5 p.m., I checked the *Post's* website and learned that you had passed away. I was devastated. You were going to be okay, I had thought. I could feel it.

As I understand it, your father had been keeping a constant vigil by your side. I'm sure he believed you'd pull through even more than I did.

I called my family and said, "She's gone." I felt empty and helpless.

My mother said, "You gave her the best chance she could have had." Perhaps. I don't think that's for me to say one way or the other.

The events of that awful day played over and over in my mind. I thought of all the things that I could have done differently. I wondered whether it would have made a difference if we could have broken out the windows and gotten you out sooner. Would a few precious moments have a made a difference? Would it have mattered if I could have gotten you into that boat a few seconds sooner? I don't know. In the end, we don't decide these things.

I can only hope that somehow you know that I did the best I could. But if I let you down, I'm sorry.

"I can't hold on…"

They say you shouldn't make these things personal. But I did. To me, it was very personal. Perhaps, in a way, I was being selfish. Perhaps I didn't only want you to be okay for your own sake, but *needed* you to be okay because I needed that validation. Is it wrong of me to feel that way?

I don't think any of these questions will ever be answered.

I know my life will never be the same. I also know that I'll never forget you. You gave me the greatest gift I've ever received. When I looked into your eyes, you became a part of me forever. And for a short period of time, you allowed me to be the kind of man I've always wanted to be: the kind that made a difference. For that, I'm eternally grateful.

Farewell, Lisa Pierce. May flocks of angels sing thee to thy rest.

With Love and Respect,

Henry Zecher, Utilityman 3rd Class
United States Naval Reserve

PS. I didn't let go

* * *

At this point I was even having trouble saying, "*wow*." When your loved ones are being admired by the world, it is just impossible to feel grief. There is only a strength and love that is propelling me to continue their efforts to help make this world a better place for everyone.

They did not leave me with sorrow. They left me with a challenge to find some small way to help change man's inhumanity to man into man's compassion for man, one person at a time, one day at a time.

Once the funerals were over I expected that things would quiet down and get back to normal. I knew that it would be a different normal than before—at least, I thought it would.

CHAPTER 8
THE TRIBUTES

Then the award presentations and memorial tributes started. The first one was for Jo Ann at Newcomb Hospital where she had worked for twenty-eight years. They had six people scheduled to speak, and when they asked if anyone else would like to say anything, six more people got up to talk about Jo Ann. This was the first time I got up in front of people to speak. Lisa loved to get up in front of people and speak, and Jo Ann was always a very good speaker. It was not something I ever did, but this year I've felt like I have been doing it all my life.

The only explanation it needs is that when Jo Ann retired from Newcomb Hospital after twenty-eight years, I was given a plaque engraved with the words, "Tom will do it," because Jo Ann was always calling me at the last minute to help her with something she forgot to do.

I have included this in the book because the day that I read it, I was wishing that I could have been reading it to all the health care workers in Baltimore that took such fantastic care of us and all the victims of that accident.

This is for all of you.

MY REMARKS AT NEWCOMB HOSPITAL

I have never been one who liked to get up in front of a group and speak. Jo Ann, on the other hand, if she had something to say—and she usually did—always wanted to say it herself, to ensure that it was communicated exactly the way she wanted it to be communicated.

I know that those of you who knew her best can picture her looking down on us today and saying what I have said over and over every time I read another beautiful story about Jo Ann or Lisa—and that is:

WOW

And she knows that the sentiments behind that "wow" will be communicated her way because,

Tom will do it

When I was in the hospital in Baltimore, one of the priests that came to see me asked how long we had been married. I told him thirty-seven years, and after a long silence I looked back at him and said, "and I have never been unhappy." Throughout this whole ordeal she is still not allowing me to be unhappy.

Your presence here today tells me that you all miss her just as much as I do. But do not allow that to make you unhappy, because that is not what she would want.

She wants you to continue to strive to achieve professionalism for yourselves and the quality of care for the patients that she always strived for when she was with us. That could never have been more evident to me than it was while we were in the hospital in Baltimore.

I felt that the level of professionalism and the compassion that they showed my family and me while we where there actually exceeded Jo Ann's standards, and I did not think that was possible.

Before we left the hospital I made them take me down to the administrator's office so I could express these feelings to him, and he could share them with all of his people. And while I was doing that, I told him a story. I told him that one day as I was walking down the hall to be with Lisa, I passed the nurses' station and overheard one of the nurses complaining to the others that, "This is not fair, they have me scheduled for every single holiday this year." And I got the biggest grin on my face because all I could think was, "Thank God I am in a real hospital, I haven't died and gone to heaven," because those types of feelings were never, ever expressed in front of me or any of my family.

These are the values that I know Jo Ann has taught us all.

These are the values that she wants us to carry with us here at Newcomb and on into the new hospital.

She knows that each and every one of you is capable of doing that.

Thank you all for being here for her today.

* * *

At the annual Community of Caring Awards Ceremony at NJIT in April they gave Lisa the Faculty/Staff service award. It was for the staff member who had tirelessly worked to build a sense of community for their campus. They also announced that in the future this award would be named after Lisa.

* * *

The next award for Jo Ann was from the Southern New Jersey Perinatal Cooperative. It included a grant for her favorite charity. Picking her favorite charity was not an easy task. On the way to Baltimore on the Friday evening before the accident Jo Ann asked me if I knew what she was the most proud of in her life. Several things came to mind, so I decided to say, "No," and let her tell me.

She said it was writing the grant that created the IMPACT Center. It was not what I expected her to say, but I totally understood her choice.

A few years ago, someone from Governor Whitman's office called and said that the Governor wanted her to write a grant for something called an IMPACT Center. It was to be a joint venture between the Board of Education and the hospital for a daycare center for children from eight weeks and up, and an education center to help students who were pregnant or had a child. She agreed but told them she could not start until the following week because we were going on vacation. They said, "No. You don't understand. In order to get this grant the Governor has to have it ready within two weeks." We actually cancelled our vacation to write this grant.

Several years ago, Jo Ann went to an anniversary celebration for the IMPACT Center and learned that Rutgers University had done a study that showed that the infants who went through the center were two years ahead of their peers because of the stimulation they received as part of the program. She also listened to a young woman who spoke eloquently about the program. She said if it were not for the program, she would have never finished high school, but now she had a scholarship to start pre-med school in September. The following year there were ten graduates and nine of them went on to college. Last year they had fifteen graduates, and when I talked to them, ten had already been accepted into college. So this year, with the help of the doctors that Jo Ann worked for and this grant, I am setting up a scholarship fund for someone who graduates from the IMPACT Center.

* * *

I heard they were going to have a medal ceremony for the reservists who rescued us that day, and I immediately knew I had to be there to thank those men. They did not invite the families of the victims, so I did not find out the date until three days before it was scheduled. I called on Thursday evening and told them I had to be there to speak to the men. I was told they would have to get permission from the commander. I showed up Saturday morning and finally got permission to speak just five minutes before the ceremony started. My remarks to those men were the first thing I wrote after the accident, and it took me all of fifteen minutes, but I think they are words that will last a lifetime.

I hope that as you finish this book you all go on to fill your lives with positive thoughts and actions so that someday I may be in total awe of each and every one of you.

MY REMARKS TO THE RESERVISTS

To Each of You,

All of you have to know how much I feel honored to be back in your presence today. A few weeks ago we all shared an extraordinary event in each of our lives. Each of us will carry our thoughts and feelings from that day with us for the rest of our lives, and those thoughts and feelings will be different for each and every one of us. When I was under that water, I did not feel the cold, or the fear, or the sense of urgency that I believe most of you felt. I said to myself, this is the day that the three of us go together, and it was a peaceful feeling. But it was not my time to leave.

I was fortunate enough to speak to both Commander Peterson Decker and Henry Zecher a few days after the accident. Both of them indicated to me that everyone who came into contact with Lisa felt that she was very special. My wife also had the ability to make people feel special. But the extent of their impact on others was far greater than even I could ever have imagined. The extent of your impact on others through this event is also far greater than I think any of you realize.

As I stood in your rescue boat and listened to the man in the wheelhouse take total command, and watched the rest of you risking your lives to get others out of the water, and then trying to breathe life back into those who needed it by doing CPR, I was in total awe of each and every one of you. Your response to this accident was absolutely magnificent.

When there is so much to be admired on that day, it becomes hard to feel the grief. I feel that both Jo Ann and Lisa are challenging each of us to try to change man's inhumanity to man into man's compassion for man, which I witnessed that day. If we could accomplish that, this world would truly be a wonderful place to live.

I know that you have all been called heroes in the past few weeks, and I am also sure that that does not make a lot of sense to you. So I am going to put it a little differently.

I would follow each and every one of you into battle.

Thank you all for being there that day.

* * *

This tribute was followed by "A Day of Remembrance" a few weeks later at Fort McHenry. It was to remember all the victims and to honor all those who helped resolve this event in so many ways. This time the mayor's office in Baltimore called me and asked if I would speak.

* * *

In September Lisa's library at NJIT was ready to be dedicated. This was such an overwhelming honor I just couldn't wait to speak at it. In just a few months I had gone from a man of very few words to someone who never missed an opportunity to speak. I truly believe this is just a part of Lisa that she left inside me.

When I first arrived at the dedication, I noticed one woman who was setting up the refreshments. I cannot explain why, but I just knew that she really missed Lisa and needed me to go over and to talk to her and give her a hug. Later that evening I told my daughter, Kathy, about it. She said, "Oh, I know the woman you're referring to. I did the same thing."

* * *

My next trip was to Stony Brook University on Long Island, where they dedicated the student lounge in the building Lisa directed eight years ago in her honor.

* * *

In October I was invited to attend the annual MACUHO conference in Wheeling, West Virginia. MACUHO stands for the Mid-Atlantic Association of College and University Housing Officers. I was invited because they were planning to honor Lisa by naming a program she created after her. Below is an article about the program that was printed in April in their international magazine, the *Talking Stick*.

LIVING A LEGACY, LEAVING A LEGACY
By John D. Stafford
April 2005

"The greatest good you can do for another is not just share your riches, but to reveal to him his own."
(Benjamin Disraeli, British Prime Minister).

Every day as higher education administrators in residence life, we work as mentors in shaping our student leaders as well as our students who are struggling with personal issues. Also along the way, we support and encourage each other, especially those on our staff. And every now and then, a person enters our life that has a profound affect on us, our careers and our professional field. Lisa A. Pierce was one of those people.

Lisa worked in residence life for almost a decade and then began work in campus activities in student leadership. Engaging students (and everyone around her) to tap into the truest self that they could create, Lisa drove students to be successful at all that they could achieve. And, along the way, she left many legacies at the institutions where she worked her magic.

Lisa was a victim of the Baltimore Water Taxi accident in March of 2004. We all lost a shining star on that day, but for our benefit, Lisa left us her legacy. On that March day Lisa's mother, Jo Ann Pierce, was also taken as a victim of the accident; her father, Tom, survived. Lisa was in Baltimore escorting students to a leadership conference, and invited her parents to spend a weekend of fun with her in the Inner Harbor. Lisa died as she lived: helping students grow and, most importantly, having some fun!

During the months following the accident, you came to see how this mother and daughter lived similar lives. Both of these women were leaders in their fields (Jo Ann worked in the medical field in South Jersey), always took care of the smallest of details, always lead with a strong will and an even bigger heart. The stories of love and compassion created enough of a legacy that any one person could hope to achieve in a lifetime, and these two women, cut from the same cloth, left a double legacy for the world.

Lisa was working at the New Jersey Institute of Technology at the time of her death, but had previously worked at Stony Brook and Russell Sage. At each of these institutions, the legacy that Lisa lived while working there has turned into a memorial legacy. Each of these institutions have dedicated lounges, libraries and memorials to her honor as a demonstration of the impact of hard work and dedication one person can achieve. Lisa's dedication to students, leadership and passion will continue to make an impression at each of these institutions.

Lisa was a passionate woman. Whether it was at work or at play, she gave a project all that she had. And most importantly, she asked for and received the same hard work and compassion from those around her. Whether you were a student working under her leadership or a colleague touched by her desire, Lisa had us all following her lead. She always made people feel important and she had a way of bringing out the best in you. Lisa treated everyone with the same level of respect, no matter who you were or what level position you held, she showed you her fun side, her caring side, her energy, her smile and laugh and those who knew her, can still hear that laugh.

This article is about one of the many legacies she created and the ongoing impact of this project, including how her father continues the legacy of both of these remarkable women.

During the spring and summer of 2001, Rider University and The College of New Jersey were selected to co-host the annual regional conference for the MACUHO (Mid Atlantic Association of College and University Housing Officers) region. The Rider/ TCNJ host committee very quickly became a New Jersey driven initiative with many from around the state joining the group. Lisa Pierce was one of those residence life go-getters that joined. When Lisa volunteered to join the committee her only "requirement" was that she be given a project to run. Early on she became the chair of the volunteer committee with a simple goal set by the group to garner enough volunteers to support the operations of the annual conference. However, Lisa had much more planned for us.

With her committee, Lisa designed a volunteer schematic that would provide the most support to the most important events at the conference. She led her group to create a volunteer force so that every subcommittee had back up support. Achieving this goal fairly quickly, Lisa set her sights to a new idea: to create a pilot program where undergraduate or graduate residence life staff at MACUHO institutions could volunteer at the conference. Lisa's outcome was very simple: to encourage growth of the residence life/student affairs field by engaging young leaders in our regional organization. During 2001 there was much conversation regionally and nationally about growing and maintaining competent professionals in our field. In true Lisa spirit she saw a need and a vehicle to get her there. A passion and vision to get the job done and grow people and our field.

Lisa created and implemented the Volunteer Incentive Program (VIP). VIP was Lisa's creative genus at work: a way to make volunteering fun at the conference, a way to provide structure to the volunteer efforts, and most importantly to her and MACUHO, an innovative way to engage undergraduate and graduate students in the housing field. Lisa played her role as a mentor from her heart as she did the creation of this program. Lisa's proposal was to recruit ten undergraduate or graduate students from MACUHO institutions, provide a waiver for their registration fees in exchange for ten hours of volunteer time. Lisa then provided the developmental mechanism to make sure that each of these volunteers was doing more than just "grunt work," but had the opportunity throughout the conference to be engaged as potential housing professionals, expose them to the field, provide networking and personally encouraging them to go to a variety of program sessions.

Lisa's idea was readily accepted by the planning group although we were concerned about how we would fund this fantastic idea. Lisa simply said, "It will happen. I will make sure." And in all Lisa created from her heart, she did. Lisa created a proposal for the MACUHO executive board, talked to whom she needed to and the MACUHO officers provided the financial support, and an idea was set to grow.

Lisa's dedication to "doing this right" with the VIP program made it the success that it was the first year and the success that is has been since. The program was such a success for the 2001 conference that the 2002 planning group moved the VIP forward for it's second year and then beginning in 2003 the MACUHO executive board moved the program to a standing committee, the Recruitment and Retention Committee. This committee's main goal is to create recruitment initiatives for the housing field and the Volunteer Incentive Program has become an annual conference force. Lisa, living a legacy, left a legacy.

With Lisa's untimely death, the host committees from 2001 and 2002 felt it was important to honor her life at the 2004 annual conference. Through a proposal to the current executive board and working with the recruitment and retention committee, a plan was created. As of the 2004 conference, the VIP has been dedicated to her honor and is now the Lisa A. Pierce Volunteer Incentive Program (Pierce VIP). Additionally, a small group of friends and colleagues put together a plan to garner support for an endowment to support and grow the program. The co-chairs of the 2001 and 2002 host committees petitioned the MACUHO executive board for a $5,000 contribution with a remaining $5,000 to be collected through fund-raising over three years, so that we could have the $10,000 minimum to create the endowment through the ACUHO-I Foundation. The executive board agreed to a $5,000 donation and plans were created to gather the other monies needed. However, Lisa's love would continue to strengthen her legacy at the annual conference.

In planning for this memorial to Lisa at the October conference, Lisa's father, Tom Pierce, was invited to attend to be present as Lisa's friends and colleagues paid tribute to her and her career. In meeting with Tom prior to the conference, we provided him with historical information on the VIP, why Lisa created the program and why it was important to her and how she lived her life. We also provided him information on what our plans were to honor his daughter. Having dinner with Tom was a very inspiring evening. Although he had lost both a daughter and his wife to this tragic accident he and his family (Lisa has a sister, brother-in-law, and two nieces) had found much solace in the discovery of the awesome work, love and legacies of these two special women. At each memorial event Tom spoke about the impact of these women and the example of "how to leave a better world behind you." Work that he saw clearly from this mother and daughter team, in their own way, to make humanity a living presence.

Tom continues this living presence by the remarks that he shared with us at the conference and by providing the Pierce Volunteer Incentive Program a growing gift. After spending time interacting with many of us at the conference, after spending time attending meals and business meetings, after engaging the current VIP group and providing us all with a laugh about our colleague, Tom provided the additional $5,000 to secure the endowment. Once more, Lisa's passion continued to grow demonstrating, over and over again, how one person's passion and idea moves forward gaining momentum and strength as each project Lisa spearheaded always did.

Lisa was the living definition of human, humane and humanitarian. At the time of the accident, many naval reservists participated in the rescue and recovery operations, one of them in a letter to Lisa and the Pierce family wrote, "Improvise, adapt, and overcome. That's what they teach you in the military. I know my life will never be the same. I also know that I'll never forget you. You gave me the greatest gift I've ever received. When I looked into your eyes, you became a part of me forever. And for a short period of time, you allowed me to be the kind of man I've always wanted to be: the kind that made a difference. For that, I'm eternally grateful."

For those of us who knew Lisa, be it student, colleague or friend, no better words could be written. She lived a legacy and she left us a legacy.

This article was written from the words, thoughts, feelings and emotions of her many colleagues and friends.

Submitted by John D. Stafford
Co-chair, 2001 MACUHO Host Committee

* * *

Each year at this conference the local school that runs it gets to pick one local charity to benefit from a basket raffle. Every school and vendor that attends brings a basket or something to raffle off. The year before the accident the conference was in Baltimore, and Towson State was the host school. Lisa's friend Becky from Stony Brook University now works at Towson and was in charge of the raffle that year. She invited Lisa down for a weekend and asked her to help her pick the local charity for that year's raffle. I have a picture of Becky's students presenting a check for $2,000 to the Living Classrooms Foundation.

Chapter 9
The Next Legacy

In January I was having dinner at a restaurant near my house where Jo Ann and I ate all the time when Dolores, one of the owners, told me they were looking for a partner so they could expand the business. Jo Ann always used to say that when she retired she would love to run a small restaurant, so I told Dolores I thought we should talk about it.

Dolores and her husband, John, and I did talk about it, and I agreed to purchase 50 percent of the business and to help them to expand. Two weeks later they had a small electrical fire in the attic of the restaurant, so they have been closed for two months. I expect that we will reopen by Mother's Day. Since the restaurant closed John has had too much time on his hands, so he went looking for a property where we could own both the building and the business. We found another property for sale and decided to buy it. My attorney asked me to meet him for lunch to sign the final papers. As he handed me the papers I became aware of the music that was playing. Music is just one more way our loved ones communicate with us. I could not begin to tell you how many people have told me similar stories this year about how specific songs are heard at very specific moments. The song playing at that moment was "To Where You Are" by Josh Groban. If you listen to the lyrics, "Can it be that you are my forever love, and are watching over me from up above," you will understand why I felt I was making the right decision.

When our second restaurant opens in October, it will be called "The Legacy," and the portraits of Jo Ann, Lisa, and Dolores' parents, who also died last year, will hang there.

Investing in a restaurant is the last thing I would have expected to do, but nothing has been normal this year. At one point I thought that, after all the memorial tributes, things would get back to normal. Now I consider normal to be a word I can no longer comprehend. Can things ever be normal after the Legacy opens? Can things ever be normal if this book actually gets published? If I really do meet someone and go on with my life, can it ever be normal? Can my life ever be normal again?

CHAPTER 10
THE SESSION

I have always been skeptical of those who refer to themselves as mediums and would never have sought out one on my own, but a friend let me listen to a tape of her session, and I decided to try it. It normally takes six to eight months to get an appointment with Ed the medium, but I told them I would go on a waitlist in case someone cancelled. Ed called me on a Sunday two weeks later, and asked if I could come in on Monday at one o'clock.

The only thing this man knew about me was that my first name was Tom. The first thing Ed said to me was, "Your father is here." He went on to explain how they use pictures and his memories to express themselves, because it requires much less energy than making specific statements to him. That allows them to communicate for a longer period of time. Then he said, "We should get started because there are at least six people here who want to talk to you."

He asked me to pick a spokesperson so they were not all talking to him at once. I picked my wife.

He said, "They are showing me a *J*, so her name must have started with a *J*." I told him her name was Jo Ann.

Then, he said, "They are taking me down I95 south to Virginia or Maryland." I told him I understood that.

"They are telling me Tom again, and I know your name is Tom. They do not usually bring up a name a second time, so what was your father's name?" I told him my father's name was Tom and he said, "Yes. He is pointing to you and saying Jr."

"Yes, I am a Jr."

"Now, wait now, he is saying one, two, three. Is there a third Tom?"

"Yes, my grandfather."

"Then wouldn't your father have been the Jr.?"

"No, they had different middle names."

He said, "Your grandfather is here, too. Now your father is showing me a picture and I know exactly what it means, but I have no idea why he wants me to tell you this. It's a picture of a pink rose with thorns coming out of it, and that means he loves you like he never could in life."

Later in the session he said, "Your father can't wait for you to get up there because he will be the father he always wanted to be." If the session had ended right then I would have been a believer, but he went on for over two hours telling me all the things that were important to them and all the times they were with Kathy and me this year.

He said, "Jo Ann is showing me a rose, and now she is showing me a small gold heart. That means that something about a rose or someone named Rose was extremely important to her."

"It's the rose," I said.

"Are you sure it's not someone named Rose, because this is something she really loved, something really big."

"It's the rose."

"Now," Ed said, "they are showing me the movie *The Wizard of Oz* and they are all singing 'Over the Rainbow.'"

He asked, "Who is Lisa?" I told him that was my daughter's name. He said they were all singing "The Wind Beneath My Wings."

Kathy was a freshman in college when that song came out. When Lisa heard it she sent it to Kathy with a beautiful letter explaining how it described her feelings for her. That year, when we all went to parent's weekend at Kathy's school, Kathy sang that song at a wine and cheese reception and dedicated it to her mother and sister.

Then he asked, "Who's inked? Who has tattoos?"

I told him the only person I knew with tattoos is Lisa's boyfriend, Karl.

He said, "Lisa wants you to tease him about the Harley."

"I don't understand that," I said.

"That's what she wants you to do."

I called Karl that night and when I told him that Lisa wanted me to tease him about the Harley, he burst into tears.

"Lisa and I were the only people on this earth who would have understood that. I called Lisa my Harley Davidson one day, and we got into a rip-roaring fight because she thought I was calling her a Hog. It took me forever to convince her that people who own Harley Davidson's love them dearly and take extra special care of them, so it finally became a term of endearment for us."

Ed asked me what was so special about August, and I told him that's when our anniversary is.

He said "Okay, now Jo Ann is showing me the number eight. Let me explain that. When they show me a number, or make me do math, I always have to add or subtract five from the number to get the final answer."

"Eight and five are thirteen, our anniversary."

"Jo Ann is moving her hands in a big square, and saying picture, picture, big picture."

"Do they like them?" I asked.

"They love them."

When the people at NJIT decided to dedicate the Leadership Development Library to Lisa, the graduate students association commissioned a painting of Lisa to hang in the library. It was just beautiful, so I contacted the artist and had a similar painting done of my wife, Jo Ann. At the time of this session the artist was finished, but I had not picked it up yet. You should have seen the artist's face when I picked up the portrait and told him how much the girls loved them!

Then Ed asked who Emily was. I told him she was my youngest granddaughter. He asked how old she was and I told him two and a half. He said, "They all want me to tell you that she talks to them all the time on her toy telephone, because no one has ever told her she can't."

I said, "I watch her do it all the time."

Then he asked who Kayla was. I said, "That's my oldest granddaughter. She is four."

He said, "Now they are showing me Britney Spears. So I am going to assume that she loves to dance and sing, and she is the artistic one of the two, isn't she?"

I told him it was the perfect description of her.

He went on to accurately describe their bedroom and the bedroom next to theirs that only has a computer in it.

As the one year anniversary approached, Tisha Thompson, from Channel 2 in Baltimore, called me and told me they were doing a story to honor the reservists and fireman who participated in the rescue. She asked if they could interview me. I told her I really did not want to be interviewed, but I would do it for them.

The camera man that day did work for both NBC and ABC. The ID badge he showed me was from NBC. So I did not realize that Channel 2 was an ABC affiliate. The next thing Ed said to me was, "Now they are showing me a peacock with all its feathers spread. So is there something about a bird, or it could be the NBC Peacock."

"NBC interviewed me on Saturday."

He said, "Wow. Now they are showing me a cruise ship or a boat."

"The interview was about the boat."

He asked me if Kayla had a friend at school by the name of Casey, and I told him I didn't know.

He said, "I think they are trying to tell me they visit her at school." When Kathy heard this, she told me that everyone at daycare calls Kayla by her initials, K.C.

These are just the highlights of my session, but I am sure you can tell how emotional my reading was that day. I felt like I had already met more than my five people from heaven. In fact, the last time I listened to the tape of my session, I wrote down the names of each person who talked to me that day. I had a list of thirteen names.

CHAPTER 11
THE ANNIVERSARY

Many people asked me what I was going to do on the first anniversary of the accident. I told them I wanted to go back to the Inner Harbor that weekend. They asked me if I was going alone. I said yes, but I did not expect to be alone.

I left Vineland around noon on Friday to go to the Harbor. The first thing I did was stop for gas. I told the attendant to fill it up. When he came back he said, "That will be thirteen dollars, even." I knew I was not traveling alone.

Not long after I checked into my hotel, I received a call from Commander Decker. He was one of the reservists who jumped in after Lisa and gave her CPR after she was back on the boat. We spoke for a long time that day. I brought him up to date on the latest tribute to Lisa at the MACUHO conference, and then I asked him how his sons were doing. He told me his oldest son just got accepted into college. I told him that Lisa always watched over her college students, and I was sure she would look after him when he went to school.

He said, "I think she is already looking out for him. I wanted to go with him the day he took his SATs, but I was supposed to go someplace with the Navy that week. When it was time for me to leave, I was sick and had to cancel, so I did get to take him. In order for him to be considered at any of the schools that he applied for, he had to take three different tests. When we arrived they told us he was only scheduled for two of the tests. I started calling people and got hold of a woman who said he could take the third test. I just had to find the principal at the school and tell him I spoke to her, and that she said to let him take the tests, and she would contact him the next day to straighten things out. As I hung up the phone the principal was walking past me. He gave my son permission to take all three tests just two minutes before the testing was scheduled to start."

Two months later, I received another call from Commander Decker. He was about to leave for Iraq. He wanted me to know that Lisa was still watching over his son. He received a scholarship to Johns Hopkins University in Baltimore, plus an additional merit scholarship.

Friday evening I met my friends from Columbia, Maryland for dinner and spent the rest of the evening with them.

The next morning I got up and went downstairs for breakfast. I have stayed at this hotel several times this year and have always ordered the breakfast buffet, but this is the first time I had breakfast alone there. When the waiter was walking over with the bill I thought, "He was very pleasant this morning. I'll leave him a three dollar tip." When I sign for a check, I have a habit of rounding the tip up to make it an even dollar amount. I left a $3.02 tip and the total bill was thirteen dollars.

After breakfast I decided to walk down to the Inner Harbor. As I crossed Light Street and stepped onto the grounds of the Harbor, I was greeted with the sounds of sirens from both a fire truck and an ambulance. I somehow thought that it was very appropriate. As I looked around to see where they were, I noticed a large banner stretched across the street announcing the Irish Parade and 5K run on March thirteenth. Lisa and Kathy loved going to the St. Patrick's Day parade in New York City every year. Once again I felt that the girls were with me every step of the way.

I followed the same basic path around the Harbor that day that we took the year before. As I started to leave I heard a small group of musicians playing music featuring a pan flute. It reminded me of the last time all four of us were in New York City together and we stopped to listen to a similar group in Times Square. I stopped and listened for a while and then went up to purchase one of their CDs, just the way I did in New York. When he sold me the disc he pointed out the song on it that they just finished playing. It was called "Women and Children." When I returned to the hotel, I read the back of the CD case. It said, "In my life other people have helped my soul sing; you, my daughter, have inspired my heart to interpret a symphony." I sincerely hope that through this book I have helped my wife and daughter inspire your life to grow to the level of a symphony that you will enjoy forever.

Two weeks later I grabbed the CD to play in the car, and as I did I realized that I had never looked at the front of the case to read the title. It was called *Angelical Inspiration*. I then slid the front cover out of the jewel case and opened it up. On the back page in large bold letters was the following quote, "I don't do big things, but I do small things with a lot of Love." If you do not think that I was inspired to buy this CD, you have not been reading this book.

At one point during my interview with Channel 2, the reporter asked me if there was anything she could do for me. I told her that I got to talk to all the reservists and even went to lunch with a few of them, and I met the two fireman that took my wife to the hospital, but I was told that another fireman jumped in to pull my wife out of the water, and I did not know his name. I asked her if she would try to find him for me while she was doing interviews for this show. His name was Bob Sebeck, and when I returned to the hotel I received a call from him. I asked if we could meet and he suggested that we meet at Hooters in the Inner Harbor. I agreed, even though I knew that my daughter Lisa never liked the philosophy behind the name of the restaurant.

I walked down to the Harbor for the second time that day to meet Bob, and as I crossed Light Street again, I was greeted by the sirens from a fire truck and an ambulance. I was the first one to arrive, and somehow I was not surprised to find that Hooters was closed for renovations. When Bob arrived we went next door to the Brew pub and talked for the next five hours. My wife always complained that I was a man of very few words. Boy would she be proud of me now. At one point during our conversation, Bob told me that he still had one son at home and that this year he started playing sports. He said he had a choice of any number he wanted on his jersey. He chose the number thirteen.

The next morning I woke up to the sound of a doorbell at 4:13 a.m. I knew that there were no doorbells in a motel so I just rolled over to go back to sleep. As I did I looked at the wall beside the bed and saw a white counter with a white towel, a bottle of wine, and two wine glasses. I just smiled and said, "I love you too," and fell back to sleep. I went to ten o'clock Mass at Father Burgess's church, but he was out of town so I did not get to talk to him. After Mass, I drove over to the armory to see if any of the reservists were there. It was completely locked up. Good thing the accident didn't happen a year later. So I went next door to Fort McHenry. I decided to start by walking down to the dock where the water taxi departed. As I approached the water, I noticed Lieutenant Commander Art Eisenstein sitting at a picnic table near the water. Art was the reservist who dove in after Sarah, the eight-year-old daughter of Dr. and Mrs. Bentrem. We spent the entire day talking about the events of the past year.

Around three o'clock I received a call from Henry Zecher, the reservist who wrote the letter to Lisa. When I hung up, Art was talking to Robert Williams and Julia Lauer, two other passengers from the water taxi. Bob and Julia and I all rode to the hospital in the same ambulance the day of the accident. Just before four o'clock, the actual time of the accident, the first mate and his wife and one of the divers and his wife arrived to share the moment with us. The diver, Bernie, told us that the following weekend would be the first anniversary of his death. He went on to explain that, just as he found Corinne Schilling's body, he got tangled in some type of long fishing line, and they had to send another diver down to rescue him. He was told that he was legally dead for six minutes, and the doctors cannot explain why he did not suffer massive brain damage. He said he has some problems but knows it was not his time. He also feels that he still has a mission to complete in this lifetime. He told us he saw his mother and other relatives as he was passing, but that they waved him back. He also told us that when he found Corinne he could hear her telling him over and over, "No! I am not ready to leave yet." He was later told that her fiancé, Andrew Roccella, was found just three feet away from where he found her. We all talked for at least another hour, and then four of us went to dinner and continued to talk until 9:30 Sunday night. Then I went back to the hotel to watch the tribute on the Channel 2 news.

Tuesday was the anniversary of Lisa's death. On Wednesday I received an e-mail from Karen Quackenbush at NJIT. She was one of the authors of Lisa's Eulogy. She told me they had a luncheon at noon in the dining room for Lisa. While Karen was greeting people at the door that day, one of the staff members came in crying. She immediately asked what was wrong, and the staff member said, "Can't you hear it." She was referring to the sounds from the clock tower that is just outside the window of Lisa's Leadership Development Library. It plays music at random each hour. At noon, it started playing "Over the Rainbow."

I wrote chapters twelve and thirteen over a month ago. Chronologically, this is the last paragraph that I intend to write.

I did not plan it this way. It just happened. Today is Jo Ann's Birthday, so this morning I bought her a rose. I was in the car after lunch and turned to the all-news radio station. I have not listened to that station in weeks. Just after I turned it on, they announced that the noon-time, pick-three Lottery number was **8–1 3**, our anniversary. I think she liked the rose. Happy birthday, Babe. I hope you like your book.

CHAPTER 12
POSITIVE THOUGHTS

Throughout this year I have talked to hundreds of people. Many of them have told me similar stories from their own lives, but others have told me that they have not seen any signs from their loved ones. I always tell these people that they have to allow themselves to be open to these signs, because I am convinced that they are always there. I try to tell them how important it is to look for the positive side of everything. Most of them tell me there is no positive side. If I can find positive things coming from the loss of my wife and daughter, then believe me, you can find the positive side of anything that happens in your life; you just have to work a little harder.

I have always felt that thought was a creative force. I recently read somewhere that "God created us through thought." Since we were created in the image and likeness of God, it makes sense to assume that our own thought process is also creative. I have always tried to force myself to think about things in a positive way. For example, when I go to a play with someone, I always ask them how they liked it. I always feel sorry for the ones who respond by saying things like, "They could have done a better job with the lighting," or, "She didn't have the best voice for the part." My responses are always about the things I liked about the play, and I always feel that I enjoyed the play more than they did. It may seem like a small thing, but I get pleasure out of feeling like I enjoy everything I do.

When I was in seventh grade I decided I wanted to take drum lessons. I talked one of my friends into starting them with me. The first day, my mother had to go with us to sign the papers. When we got there they told us the teacher was late. So, while my mother was filling out the papers, Bob and I wandered around the store. We looked at everyone who came in, wondering if they would be our new teacher. Finally, a little man in a black overcoat came in and went up to the counter. He had bad skin and teeth, was chicken-breasted, and hunch-backed. Bob and I looked at each other and said, "Oh God, I hope it's not him." I think we both thought he might be the ugliest man we had ever seen. He was standing next to my mother at the counter. When she turned and saw him, she exclaimed "Charlie" and gave him a big hug. My eyes were bugging out of my head. Bob looked at me and said, "Who is that?" I shrugged and told him I had no idea. My mother introduced him as someone she grew up with, and we followed Charlie upstairs for our first drum lesson.

After just one hour with this man, I could not wait to get home to talk to my mother about him. I wanted to know everything about him, and Bob made me promise to call him as soon as I finished so I could fill him in. My mother told me that Charlie lived in her neighborhood and that his parents owned the bakery. She said that he always had health problems, and his parents spent a fortune in medical expenses for him. She went on to say that he had the nicest personality of anyone she had ever met and that he was always the life of the party. She never knew he played drums, because when he came to the house he would bring his fiddle and they would all have a great time. Then she told me that he was married to the most beautiful girl in the neighborhood, because no one could resist his positive attitude.

I took lessons from Charlie for almost five years and still consider him to be the most beautiful man I have ever met. Charlie was an outstanding music teacher, but he taught more about love, understanding, acceptance, and overcoming adversity than he ever taught about music. I still miss him. No one would have doubted that Charlie felt that positive thoughts were creative. No one will ever convince me that positive thoughts are not creative. Don't ever let anyone convince you that your positive thoughts will not be creative.

CHAPTER 13
THE LEGACY OF LOVE

I hope it is obvious to you by now that many, many things have happened for me this past year—little things but, as I said in the beginning, in numbers there is strength. I have been a computer programmer all of my life, and logic has always played a big part in the way that I think. I believe that the events I have outlined in this book truly defy logic—at least logic as we observe it on our human plane. The only logical explanation for all of these things is that there really is a spiritual plane of existence that is totally outside our realm of comprehension. I have found this realization to be very comforting. But what I have found to be the most comforting is the realization of just how much of a difference we as individuals can make in this world, just by trying to live our lives being the best that we can be. Not the best that we can be for our own sake, but the best we can be for each other.

When Jo Ann and I were driving home from our honeymoon, the oil pump in my car went bad and we had to be towed to a garage and stay overnight in a motel while it was being repaired. When we got back on the road the next day, we only drove another hour when my fuel pump went. As we coasted to the side of the road, I think we were both ready to cry, but almost immediately a man pulled over behind us and asked us what the problem was. My first thoughts were, "Who the heck is this clown, and how am I going to deal with him?" He went on to explain that he was a mechanic, and he would take a look at the problem and try to help because it was Sunday, and he did not know of anyone in the area who was open that could help us. He actually spent several hours that day getting us back on the road, and when I tried to pay him he said, "No. But when you see someone else in trouble and you think you can help, just do it for me."

I do not know his name, but I have never forgotten him, or his philosophy. There have been many times in the past thirty-eight years that I have tried to emulate his kindness. Hopefully I have convinced many of you to emulate the ideals expressed throughout this book, because each time we make a difference in someone else's life, no matter how small, it will encourage them to do the same for others. And each time that happens, we all become a stronger force for good. When the time comes that we all base our actions on love and compassion for all mankind, there will be no need for war or weapons. It only requires a small effort from each of us to accomplish what may seem impossible. It just requires all of us to do it together.

A few years ago, Lisa was home for the weekend, and while we were driving to the store together she asked me if I was okay. I said, "Yes. Why?" She said, "Mom told me you went to the doctor last week, and I want to know if every thing is all right." I told her everything was fine. It was just an annual checkup. She said, "Are you sure? Because I love my daddy and I don't know what I would do if anything happened to you." Then she started to cry. I said, "Lisa! Wrong attitude! I am fine, but even if I wasn't, you have to realize that if I died tomorrow I would die a happy man. I have been married for over thirty years and have always felt that I had the greatest marriage that anyone could ever ask for. I have two beautiful children who have never given me anything but pure pleasure in this life. I am sure that if anything ever happened to me you would be very sad, but don't ever allow that to make you unhappy." As they closed her casket for the last time, I told her that it wasn't supposed to happen in this sequence, but I would always love her, and I would miss her. Then I promised her I would not allow myself to have the wrong attitude, because I knew she loved life just as much as I did.

I could never count the number of tears I shed while writing this book, and I think that anyone who reads this book might find themselves sharing a few of their tears with me along the way. But I think that it is important to realize that these are tears of joy, not sorrow; tears of laughter, not pain; tears of love, not grief.

Tears are a way that our bodies help us cope with things that are beyond our comprehension. It is important that we all share our tears with each other so that we can emerge as stronger individuals ready to make this world a better place for everyone.

Those of you who have read the eulogies of these women will understand why I think that both of their lives can be summed up in one sentence.

All the kindness a person puts out into the world works on the hearts and thoughts of mankind.

Those of you who have read this book from start to finish will understand why I think the whole point of this book can be summarized in one sentence. For those of you who always read the ending of a book first, I can only hope that this one sentence captures your hearts and minds enough to compel you to read this book from start to finish.

To truly love someone and be loved in return is to see the face of God.

Love Always,

Tom
Thelastrose@comcast.net